## THE NEWCOMERS SERIES

# AFRICAN AMERICANS IN U.S. HISTORY

## 1877 TO THE PRESENT

## VOLUME 2

**GLOBE BOOK COMPANY**
Englewood Cliffs, N.J.

## USING SOCIAL STUDIES SKILLS

**Front cover, clockwise:** Dr Martin Luther King, Jr, Mary McLeod Bethune,
George Washington Carver, Sojourner Truth
**Cover art:** Alan J. Nahigian
**Design:** Function Thru Form, Inc.
**Photo research:** Omni-Photo Communications, Inc.

Printed in the United States of America

10 9 8 7 6 5 4 3 2 1

ISBN 1–55675–589–9

Globe Book Company
A Division of Simon & Schuster
Englewood Cliffs, New Jersey

# C O N T E N T S

To the student: The notes printed in red in Chapter 1 will help you get started on Blacks in American History, Volume 2.

# THE BETRAYAL OF BLACK RIGHTS

Chapter **1**

**AIM: How did the Jim Crow system arise in the South? What rights were denied Blacks under this system?**

Read the text to answer the AIM question(s).

1. The period after the Civil War is called **Reconstruction.** It lasted from 1865 to 1877. In this time, the South was rebuilt. Blacks made many gains during the first years of Reconstruction. However, they gradually lost these gains. New state laws set up a system of **segregation**, or separation of Blacks and Whites. This system was known as **"Jim Crow."** The name came from a song that pictured Blacks as inferior and childlike. Throughout the South, laws separated Blacks and Whites on streetcars and trains, in theaters and schools, and even in graveyards.

2. The Supreme Court supported segregation. In 1883, it struck down the Civil Rights Act of 1875. This law made it a crime to segregate Blacks and Whites in hotels, trains, and other public places. In 1896, Homer Plessy, a Black man, sued to overturn a Louisiana law. This law required Blacks and Whites to sit in separate cars on railroad trains. In the case of *Plessy v. Ferguson*, the Supreme Court ruled

The first sentence in each paragraph gives the main idea.

▲ These boys and girls are students in an all-Black school in Athens, Georgia, around 1890.

The caption will help you understand the illustration.

against Plessy. It said segregation was legal if the facilities were "separate but equal." One Supreme Court justice, John Marshall Harlan, **dissented**, or disagreed with this decision. He wrote, "Our Constitution is color-blind."

Vocabulary words are defined in context near and are also found in the Glossary.

3. In practice, the "separate" part of the "separate but equal" idea was carried out, but the "equal" part was not. Passenger cars for Blacks on trains were uncomfortable, dirty, and noisy. States spent less money on schools for Blacks than they did on White schools. Conditions for Blacks were not much better after the Plessy decision than they had been before.

4. The southern states also passed laws to keep Blacks from voting. In many of the states, people had to pay a **poll tax**. This was a fee a person had to pay in order to vote. Most Blacks could not afford to pay the poll tax. Therefore, they could not vote. In some places, voters had to pass literacy tests. These tests required voters to be able to read and understand parts of the state constitution. Few people, Whites as well as Blacks, could pass such a test. The "grandfather clause" protected White political power. The grandfather clause allowed people to vote if their ancestors had the right to vote before 1867. Only Whites in the South could vote before 1867. Jim Crow ended Black political power in the South. The last Black Congressman from the South was elected in 1898.

5. Blacks also faced insulting treatment to "keep them in their place." Whites called Black men by their first names, or simply "boy." More seriously, White mobs spread fear among Blacks through killings called **lynchings**. From 1882 to 1900, around 2,000 Black Americans were lynched.

6. Most northerners did not protest the Jim Crow system. Indeed, racist attitudes were almost as strong in the North as in the South. Magazines and newspapers carried cartoons that made fun of Blacks. Labor unions, which were growing at this time, would not accept Blacks as members. Thus, Blacks faced an increasingly hostile world.

**Study tip** To review, reread the first sentence in each paragraph. Also review the time chart on the back cover.

# Understanding What You Have Read

Check your comprehension by doing these activities.

**A.** Write the words that best complete each sentence in the space provided.

Jim Crow laws     John Marshall Harlan     grandfather clause
Reconstruction     Homer Plessy

1. _____ tried to overturn a law that made Blacks and Whites use separate railroad cars.

2. _____ was the judge who dissented from the Supreme Court's decision in the case of *Plessy v. Ferguson*.

3. The _____ said that persons could vote if their ancestors could vote before 1867.

4. _____ was the period after the Civil War when the South was rebuilt.

5. _____ set up a system of segregation of the races.

**B.** In each of the sentences that follow, the underlined word or words make the sentence true or false. If the sentence is true, write **T** in the blank before it. If it is false, write the word or words that make the sentence true.

_____ 1. After Reconstruction, state governments in the South tried to <u>protect</u> the rights of blacks.

_____ 2. In the case of *Plessy v. Ferguson*, the Supreme Court said that this system of segregation was <u>legal</u>.

_____ 3. To protect the Jim Crow system, laws were passed to let only <u>Blacks</u> vote.

_____ 4. In the South, only the "<u>separate</u>" part of the "separate but equal" idea was usually carried out.

Each chapter has one of these activities: **Building Geography Skills, Linking Past to Present,** or **Daily Life.**

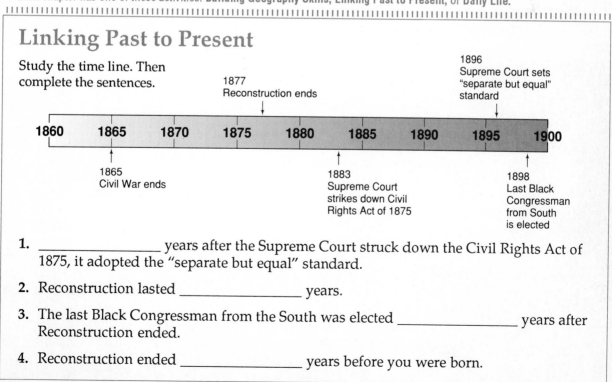

## Linking Past to Present

Study the time line. Then complete the sentences.

1. _____ years after the Supreme Court struck down the Civil Rights Act of 1875, it adopted the "separate but equal" standard.

2. Reconstruction lasted _____ years.

3. The last Black Congressman from the South was elected _____ years after Reconstruction ended.

4. Reconstruction ended _____ years before you were born.

# Spotlight on People

**Ida Wells.** No one was a greater foe of Jim Crow and lynching than Ida Wells. Born a slave in Holly Springs, Mississippi, in 1862, she was orphaned at sixteen. Yet she managed to support her brothers and sisters and get an education. Wells moved to Memphis, where she became a schoolteacher.

In 1884, she was ordered to leave the first-class section of a train. When she refused, she was removed by force. Wells sued the railroad company and won her case. The train company appealed the case to the Tennessee Supreme Court, and Wells lost. Because of her lawsuit, Ida Wells lost her teaching job. She then found a job on a Black newspaper and became its editor.

After a close friend was lynched in 1892, Wells began a lifelong crusade against this terrible practice. She called for Blacks to boycott, or refuse to shop at, White businesses. She defended Blacks' right to protect themselves: "When the White man . . . knows he runs as great a risk of biting the dust every time his Afro-American victim does, he will have greater respect for Afro-American life." After her newspaper accused Whites of the lynching, a White mob smashed her newspaper office.

In 1895, Ida Wells wrote a book called *A Red Record* to show how widespread the practice of lynching had become. She worked tirelessly to awaken the public to the problem. She traveled and spoke throughout the United States and overseas. She was active in the founding of the National Association for the Advancement of Colored People in 1909. Wells settled in Chicago, where she married Ferdinand Barnett, a lawyer and journalist. Until her death in 1931, Ida Wells continued to oppose segregation in all its forms.

## Recalling the Facts

Choose each correct answer and write the letter in the space provided.

_____ 1. Ida Wells became involved with the struggle for Black rights when
    **a.** her parents died.
    **b.** she was turned down by a college.
    **c.** she was forced to leave a Whites-only railroad car.

_____ 2. Wells began her crusade against lynching after
    **a.** a close friend was lynched.
    **b.** President McKinley urged her to.
    **c.** she lost her teaching job.

_____ 3. A mob attacked Ida Wells' newspaper office because
    **a.** she would not defend herself.
    **b.** she accused Whites of lynching.
    **c.** she would not support a White candidate.

_____ 4. Wells believed one way Blacks could fight back was to
    **a.** call the police.
    **b.** boycott White businesses.
    **c.** take their case to the Supreme Court.

_____ 5. To spread her anti-lynching crusade, Wells
    **a.** stayed within the South.
    **b.** left the United States for good.
    **c.** traveled throughout the United States and abroad.

# Using Primary Sources

After the Civil War, Sojourner Truth became active in the struggle to gain full equality for both Blacks and women. A White friend of Sojourner's wrote her life story. The following selection describes Sojourner's attempts to allow Blacks on the horse-drawn streetcars of Washington, D.C.

Mrs. Laura Haviland, a White, sometimes went about the city with Sojourner. Mrs. Haviland proposed to take a streetcar, although she was well aware that a White person was seldom allowed to ride if accompanied by a Black one. Sojourner said: "A man coming out as we were going into the next car asked the conductor if 'colored were allowed to ride.' The conductor grabbed me by the shoulder and jerking me around, ordered me out. I told him I would not. Mrs. Haviland took hold of my other arm and said, 'Don't put her out.' The conductor asked if I belonged to her. 'No,' replied Mrs. Haviland. 'She belongs to humanity.' 'Then take her and go,' said he, and giving me another push slammed me against the door. I told him I would let him know whether he could shove me about like a dog, and said to Mrs. Haviland, 'Take the number of this car.'

At this, the man looked alarmed, and gave us no more trouble. When we arrived at the hospital where Mrs. Haviland worked, the surgeons were called to examine my shoulder and found that a bone was misplaced. I complained to the president of the streetcar company, who advised me to arrest the man for assault and battery. The Bureau furnished me a lawyer, and the conductor lost his job. Before the trial was ended, the inside of cars looked like pepper and salt. A little story will show how great a change a few weeks had produced: A lady saw some colored women looking wistfully toward a car, when the conductor, halting, said, "Walk in, ladies." Now they who had so lately cursed me for wanting to ride, could stop for Black as well as White, and could even condescend to say, "Walk in, ladies."

1.  What happened when Sojourner Truth tried to ride on a streetcar with her White friend? _____
    _____

2.  What were the results of Sojourner Truth's lawsuit against the streetcar conductor?
    _____

Critical Thinking helps you think about what you have read and puts the chapter into historical perspective.

## CHAPTER REVIEW: CRITICAL THINKING ▮▮▮

1.  Toward the end of his life, Frederick Douglass wrote: "Though slavery was abolished, the wrongs of my people were not ended. Though they were not slaves, they were not yet quite free." In what ways were Blacks "not yet quite free"? _____
    _____

2.  What can you learn from Sojourner Truth's actions in the streetcar incidents? _____
    _____

# BLACKS RESPOND TO JIM CROW

**AIM: What did Blacks do to fight Jim Crow? Why did some Blacks believe they should accept Jim Crow?**

1. Blacks fought the Jim Crow system in different ways. In some places, they started **boycotts**. In a boycott, people refuse to buy or use someone's goods or services in order to influence that person. In Atlanta, Blacks boycotted the streetcars. The boycott succeeded, and Blacks were allowed to ride with the Whites. A Black writer, T. Thomas Fortune, said that Blacks had to fight their own battles. "It is time to face the enemy," he wrote, "and fight inch by inch for every right he denies us."

2. **Prejudice** and poverty in the South caused some Blacks to leave and look for a better life. They went to cities in both the North and the South. With the Black population in cities growing, Black-owned businesses sprang up. Blacks started their own insurance companies because many White companies would not insure Blacks. Blacks also started their own banks and stores.

▲ Booker T. Washington believed that Blacks should be trained in practical skills. In this way, he said, Blacks could advance and gain the respect of Whites.

3. Some Blacks felt that they should even start their own communities. In the 1870s, Benjamin "Pap" Singleton thought Blacks should move to a "freedom land" in Kansas. In 1879, he organized what he called a "colored **exodus**," or departure. Those who followed him were called **Exodusters**. Edwin P. McCabe tried to make Oklahoma an all-Black territory. Although he failed, some all-Black Oklahoma towns arose between 1889 and 1910. One such town was Boley. It had a high school, a telephone system, and over 80 businesses. Boley showed what Blacks could do when they were free from the system of discrimination.

4. Some Blacks moved West. They did many different kinds of work. Some worked on ranches and took part in the great cattle drives. Others served in the army in the Indian wars. Among them was the first Black graduate of West Point, Henry Flipper. Some Blacks became allies of the Indians. A Black called John Horse led Apache Indians against United States troops.

5. In the 1890s, one person became the chief spokesperson for Blacks. He was Booker T. Washington. Born a slave, Washington was educated at Hampton Institute in Hampton, Virginia. In 1881, he founded Tuskegee Institute in Alabama. Tuskegee gave Blacks a practical education. It taught trades and scientific methods of farming. Washington urged Blacks not to fight the Jim Crow system. Instead, he said, they should improve themselves through vocational education. Then when they were prepared, they should seek full rights.

6. Washington became famous overnight after a speech he made in Atlanta in 1895. He said Blacks should not take part in politics or move out of "our beloved South." He brought the mostly White crowd to its feet by saying, "In all things that are purely social we can be as separate as the fingers, yet one as the hand in all things essential to mutual progress." Washington's message brought him and his school the support of wealthy and powerful Whites. For years, he was thought of as the leader of Black Americans.

## Understanding What You Have Read

**A.** Fill in the blank in each sentence with the name below that best completes the sentence.

Booker T. Washington      T. Thomas Fortune      John Horse
Henry Flipper      Benjamin "Pap" Singleton

1. _____ tried to persuade Blacks to move to Kansas.

2. _____ said that Blacks had to fight their own battles.

3. _____ was the first Black graduate of West Point.

4. _____ said that Blacks should not try to fight the Jim Crow system.

5. _____ led Apaches against the United States army.

**B.** Write the letter of the best answer in the blank next to each sentence.

_____ **1.** The main idea of paragraph 1 is
   **a.** Blacks needed help to fight the Jim Crow system.
   **b.** Many Blacks tried to fight the Jim Crow system on their own.
   **c.** T. Thomas Fortune was opposed to the Jim Crow system.

_____ **2.** The main topic of paragraph 3 is
   **a.** the life of Benjamin "Pap" Singleton.
   **b.** Blacks' acceptance of the Jim Crow system in the South.
   **c.** Blacks' attempts to settle in Kansas and Oklahoma.

_____ **3.** From the information in paragraph 3, you know that Boley, Oklahoma,
   **a.** was a failed attempt at Black settlement.
   **b.** showed that Blacks could be successful in a system without prejudice.
   **c.** did not last after 1910.

_____ **4.** Paragraph 6 tells you
   **a.** Booker T. Washington's reasons for starting Tuskegee Institute.
   **b.** how Booker T. Washington got his education.
   **c.** Booker T. Washington's ideas about what Blacks should do about Jim Crow.

## Building Geography Skills

Study the map on this page. Then complete the sentences.

1. The number of Blacks in the South was _____ in 1900 than in 1860.

2. The region with the smallest number of Blacks in 1860 and 1900 was the _____.

3. The region with the greatest gain in percentage of Blacks from 1860 to 1900 was the _____ region.

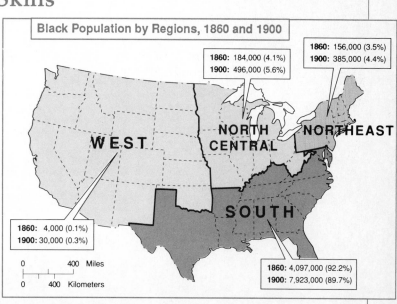

**Black Population by Regions, 1860 and 1900**

**1860:** 156,000 (3.5%)
**1900:** 385,000 (4.4%)

**1860:** 184,000 (4.1%)
**1900:** 496,000 (5.6%)

WEST

NORTH CENTRAL

NORTHEAST

SOUTH

**1860:** 4,000 (0.1%)
**1900:** 30,000 (0.3%)

**1860:** 4,097,000 (92.2%)
**1900:** 7,923,000 (89.7%)

0      400   Miles

0      400   Kilometers

# Spotlight on People

**Sarah Breedlove.** Sarah Breedlove was the first woman of any race who ever earned a million dollars. Born in Louisiana, she grew up in St. Louis. There she worked as a laundress to support her daughter and herself. At night, Breedlove attended school. As she later recalled, she worried because her hair was falling out. In a dream, an old man told her "what to mix up for my hair." She ordered the things the old man told her about. She found they worked. "My hair was coming in faster than it had ever fallen out," she claimed. "I tried it on my friends. It helped them. I made up my mind that I would begin to sell it."

Breedlove began selling her hair product door to door. She soon saw that there was a demand for beauty products for Blacks. She created a line of cosmetics and opened beauty parlors under the name "Madame C. J. Walker." In 1910, Breedlove built a factory to make hair preparations and face creams. Soon Madame C. J. Walker's beauty salons were found throughout the United States, the Caribbean, and South America. She started a school to train workers in the "Walker system" of beauty care. By 1910, the Walker Company had sales of $1,000 a day and 5,000 saleswomen around the world.

Sarah Breedlove was now a wealthy woman. She bought a house in Harlem and built a mansion on the Hudson River. She bought one of the expensive electric automobiles that were popular in the early 1900s. The picture on this page shows her driving the car. She gave generously to Black causes. She was particularly interested in education and women's welfare. At her death in 1919, she left two-thirds of her fortune to charity. Her will required that the head of the Walker Company always be a woman.

## Recalling the Facts

Choose each correct answer and write the letter in the space provided.

_____ 1. Sarah Breedlove's first beauty product was
   a. a face cream.
   b. a preparation to keep hair from falling out.
   c. a spray to keep hair in place.

_____ 2. Breedlove began to sell her products
   a. by going door to door.
   b. through a local beauty parlor.
   c. through the mail.

_____ 3. Breedlove as "Madame C. J. Walker" was successful because
   a. she spent her profits only on her business.
   b. other businesspeople lent her money.
   c. she saw the need for beauty products especially made for Blacks.

_____ 4. Breedlove opened a school
   a. so that others would not have to struggle to earn a living.
   b. to train new workers in her system of beauty care.
   c. whenever she started a new beauty parlor.

# Using Primary Sources

When Nat Love was 15, he left his father's farm in Tennessee and went West. He worked on ranches in Texas and Arizona. As a Black cowboy, he became famous for his skills at riding and shooting. He published his life story in 1907. In this selection Love tells how he got the nickname "Deadwood Dick."

The conditions of the contest were that each of us who were mounted was to rope, throw, tie, bridle and saddle, and mount the particular horse picked for us in the shortest time possible. The man accomplishing the feat in the quickest time [was] to be declared the winner.

It seems to me that the horse chosen for me was the most vicious of the lot. Everything being in readiness, the "45" [starting pistol] cracked and we all sprang forward together, each of us making for our particular mustang.

I roped, threw, tied, bridled, saddled, and mounted my mustang in exactly nine minutes from the crack of the gun. The time of the next nearest competitor was twelve minutes and thirty seconds.

This gave me the record and championship of the West, which I held up to the time I quit the business in 1890, and my record has never been beaten. It is worthy of passing remark that I never had a horse pitch with me so much as that mustang, but I never stopped sticking my spurs in him and using my quirt on his flanks until I proved his master. Right there the assembled crowd named me Deadwood Dick and proclaimed me champion roper of the western cattle country.

▲ Nat Love was one of the Black cowboys of the West.

## Vocabulary

**mustang** a small wild horse    **quirt** whip    **flanks** sides

1. What did the cowboys have to do to win the contest? _____

   _____

2. What title did Nat Love win in the contest? _____

# CHAPTER REVIEW: CRITICAL THINKING ▬▬▬

Though they faced poverty and prejudice in the South, most Blacks did not choose to move to other places. What reasons might they have had for staying where they were?

_____

_____

# Chapter 3 ACHIEVEMENTS AND HOPES

**AIM: What were the achievements of Blacks in the period after Reconstruction? Where did they make contributions?**

1. It is said that without Blacks, there would be no truly American music. The music that sprang from Black roots has been one of the most important contributions of the United States to world culture. To create this music, Blacks drew on both their African heritage and American experiences. From Africa came the rhythms and the use of music in daily life.

2. Many Blacks adopted the Christian religion. They created songs called **spirituals** to express their religious feelings. After the Civil War, students at Fisk University in Nashville, Tennessee, formed a choir called the Fisk Jubilee Singers. They toured the United States and Europe, singing spirituals to enthusiastic audiences.

3. Work songs were also part of Black music. The strong rhythms of these songs came from the movements of workers in the fields.

▲ The Fisk Jubilee Singers introduced spirituals to audiences in the United States and Europe. The money they earned helped Fisk University, in Nashville, Tennessee, put up many of its buildings.

One example is "John Henry," which told the story of a real person who worked on the West Virginia Railroad in the 1880s. City workers made up their own work songs. Many of them were sung by peddlers as they sold their goods in the street.

4. Another type of Black music is the **blues**. Spirituals and work songs were generally sung in groups. The blues were sung by individuals. Blues songs told of a person's own sadness and unhappiness.

5. Blacks made important contributions to other American industries. In 1883, Jan Matzeliger invented a machine that attached the upper part of a shoe to the lower part. Soon, his invention was used for making almost all the shoes in the United States. Another Black inventor, Granville T. Woods, made improvements in the telephone and telegraph. Lewis Howard Latimer invented an early type of light bulb in 1881. Latimer later worked with Thomas A. Edison to install the first electric lighting systems in New York, Philadelphia, and London, England.

6. In 1893, Dr. Daniel Hale Williams became the first surgeon to operate successfully on the human heart. Doctors came from all over the country to learn to perform the operation. Williams' Chicago hospital was the first in the country to accept patients of all races. Black doctors and nurses were trained there. Williams helped start over 40 Black hospitals in 20 states.

7. There were many Black writers in the late 1800s. These included Paul Laurence Dunbar, the poet, and Charles W. Chesnutt, the first popular Black novelist. Booker T. Washington's autobiography, or life story, *Up From Slavery*, was a best-seller. George Washington Williams wrote the first important history of American Blacks. Williams said he hoped to help the day come "when there shall be no North, no South, no Black, no White— but all American citizens with equal duties and equal rights."

A. Match the items in the second column with the names in the first column.

| | | |
|---|---|---|
| _____ **1.** Jan Matzeliger | | **a.** wrote a history of American Blacks. |
| _____ **2.** Granville T. Woods | | **b.** was the first surgeon to operate on the human heart. |
| _____ **3.** Lewis Howard Latimer | | **c.** invented an early light bulb. |
| _____ **4.** Daniel Hale Williams | | **d.** invented a machine for making shoes. |
| _____ **5.** Paul Laurence Dunbar | | **e.** was the first popular Black novelist. |
| _____ **6.** George Washington Williams | | **f.** made improvements for telephones and telegraphs. |
| _____ **7.** Charles W. Chesnutt | | **g.** introduced Black spirituals to White audiences. |
| _____ **8.** The Fisk Jubilee Singers | | **h.** was a famous Black poet. |

B. Fill in the blank with the term that best completes the sentence.

blues songs    work song    rhythms    spirituals

1. "John Henry" is an example of a Black _____.

2. The _____ of Black music came from African songs.

3. Religious songs were known as _____.

4. _____ were about personal sadness.

## Daily Life

**The Cakewalk.** Dances as well as music have been part of the everyday life of Blacks from the earliest days. As with music, the dances of Blacks have become part of the mainstream of American life.

One of the earliest of such dances was the tap dance. Later came the **cakewalk.** This dance got its name from the fact that the couple that performed the dance best won a cake as a prize. In the cakewalk, couples did high kicks, leaps, and complicated turns. The dance made fun of the manners of wealthy White society. The liveliness of the cakewalk attracted White dancers. At the end of the 1800s, it swept the United States and Europe as a favorite dance.

▲ In the cakewalk, the dancers poke fun at the dances of wealthy Whites.

1. How did the cakewalk get its name? _____

2. Why did it become popular in the United States and Europe? _____

_____

# Spotlight on People

**Paul Laurence Dunbar.** Dunbar was the first Black poet who became well known throughout the United States. Born in Dayton, Ohio, in 1872, Dunbar started writing poems at age 6. He was the only Black in his high school class, but his teachers saw his talent. They encouraged him to write poems. He could not afford to go to college. Newspapers would not hire him because of his race. So, Dunbar worked as an elevator operator and wrote poems in his spare time.

Dunbar paid $125 to have a book of his poems printed. He sold copies to passengers on his elevator. Some of them helped him to bring out a second book. A famous White writer, William Dean Howells, saw the book and praised it in his magazine. Soon Dunbar's work became known throughout the country. Besides his poems, he wrote songs, novels, and short stories. He traveled the country, giving readings from his work.

Dunbar's life was tragically short. He died of tuberculosis at age 33. Today, one of the largest high schools in Dayton, Ohio, is named after him. Here is one of Dunbar's poems.

## We Wear the Mask

We wear the mask that grins and lies,
It hides our cheeks and shades our eyes,—
This debt we pay to human guile;
With torn and bleeding hearts we smile,
And mouth with myriad subtleties.

Why should the world be overwise,
In counting all our tears and sighs?
Nay, let them only see us, while
   We wear the mask.

We smile, but, O great Christ, our cries
To Thee from tortured souls arise.
We sing, but oh, the clay is vile
Beneath our feet, and long the mile;
But let the world dream otherwise,
   We wear the mask.

## Vocabulary

**guile** deceit, cunning     **myriad** many     **subtleties** hidden meanings

## Recalling the Facts

Choose each correct answer and write the letter in the space provided.

_____ 1. Dunbar began writing poems
   a. at age six.
   b. in high school.
   c. after he worked as an elevator operator.

_____ 2. Dunbar's first book of poems
   a. brought him nationwide fame.
   b. was paid for by Dunbar himself.
   c. never sold any copies.

_____ 3. Dunbar was helped by a
   a. White writer.
   b. wealthy woman.
   c. Black doctor.

# The Arts and Technology

**Science.** George Washington Carver, who was born a slave in 1864, became one of this country's greatest scientists. His discoveries helped to change farming in the South. He could have become rich from his work. Yet he offered his discoveries free to all.

Before Carver, the South's agriculture was a "one-crop economy." That is, most of its farmland was used for growing cotton. However, years of cotton crops wore out the soil. Carver knew that planting other crops would help the soil recover. Among these plants were sweet potatoes, peanuts, and soybeans. However, none of them brought as high prices as cotton, so farmers would not plant them. Carver set out to find ways to make use of these plants to encourage farmers to plant them.

Through his experiments, Carver found more than 300 uses for the peanut. Among them were peanut butter, dyes, wood stain, and insulating material. From the sweet potato he developed a kind of flour. It became an important food source during World War I. Among more than 100 other sweet-potato products was a glue for postage stamps. He also developed products

▲ George Washington Carver with one of his students in the laboratory of Tuskegee Institute.

from the clay of the South and was the first to use soybeans in the making of paint. Carver's work benefitted the entire South by helping to change the one-crop economy for good.

He also discovered ways to fight plant diseases. When Carver died in 1943, he was the most respected agricultural scientist in the country. The Carver National Monument, near his birthplace, was the first national monument to honor a Black.

1. Farmland in the South was worn out because _____

_____

2. Carver looked for new uses for peanuts, soybeans, and sweet potatoes because

_____

3. Carver's work benefitted the South by _____

_____

## CHAPTER REVIEW: CRITICAL THINKING

1. In the period after Reconstruction, White-owned newspapers and magazines showed Blacks as ignorant and childlike. What evidence do you find in the chapter that this was a false

   picture of Blacks? _____

   _____

2. How do you think the treatment of Blacks would have been different if their achievements

   were better known? _____

   _____

# UNIT 1 REVIEW

## Summary of the Unit

A few of the most important events and facts presented in Unit 1 are listed below. Write these events and facts in your notebook and add three more.

1. After Reconstruction, southern Whites passed laws to restrict the rights of Blacks.
2. Some of these laws created a system in which Whites and Blacks were separated, or segregated. The system was called Jim Crow.
3. Blacks tried to fight this system. Some began their own communities in the West.
4. Booker T. Washington, a Black leader, advised Blacks not to fight the Jim Crow system.
5. Despite the prejudice against them, Blacks had many achievements in the period after Reconstruction.

## Understanding What You Have Read

Write the letter of the answer that best completes each sentence in the space provided.

_____ 1. The Supreme Court
    a. opposed segregation.
    b. supported segregation.
    c. did not rule on segregation laws.

_____ 2. White southerners kept Blacks from winning elections
    a. by preventing Blacks from voting.
    b. by sending Blacks to other areas.
    c. by not allowing Blacks to run for office.

_____ 3. Blacks left the South to go West
    a. to find better weather.
    b. because no Whites lived in the West.
    c. to escape prejudice.

_____ 4. Booker T. Washington
    a. was popular only among Whites.
    b. was popular only among Blacks.
    c. thought vocational education was best for Blacks.

_____ 5. The sources of Black music were
    a. both African and American.
    b. only African.
    c. only American.

_____ 6. Black inventors
    a. were unsuccessful because Blacks had little education.
    b. were successful in a variety of fields.
    c. could not sell their inventions because of prejudice.

## Building Your Vocabulary

Choose one of the words below to complete each of the following sentences.

exodus    blues    boycott    lynching
segregation    dissent    spiritual

_____ 1. Separation of the races is called _____.

_____ 2. To _____ from something is to disagree with it.

_____ 3. A _____ is the refusal of many people to buy or use something.

_____ 4. An _____ is the movement of a group of people out of a region or country.

_____ 5. A _____ is a religious song that tells a story or expresses feeling.

_____ 6. A _____ song expresses personal sorrow.

_____ 7. A _____ is the killing of Blacks by White mobs.

## Developing Ideas and Skills—Understanding a Chart

Study the chart. Then decide whether each statement is true. If the statement is true, write **T** next to it. If it is false, write **F**. Then rewrite the statement to make it true.

### Black Population of the United States

| Year | Number of Blacks | Number of Whites | % of Blacks |
|------|------------------|------------------|-------------|
| 1870 | 5,392,172 | 39,818,449 | 13.5 |
| 1880 | 6,580,973 | 50,155,783 | 13.1 |
| 1890 | 7,488,676 | 62,974,714 | 11.9 |
| 1900 | 8,833,994 | 175,944,575 | 11.6 |

_____ 1. In each ten-year period on the chart, the total number of Blacks decreased.

_____

_____

_____ 2. The chart shows how many Blacks in 1870 were ex-slaves.

_____

_____

_____ 3. The number of Whites almost doubled from 1870 to 1900.

_____

_____

_____ 4. The percentage of Blacks in the United States increased between 1870 and 1890.

_____

_____

## Making History Live

1. In one of his speeches, Booker T. Washington advised Blacks to "Cast down your bucket where you are." In your notebook, explain what he meant. Tell how the statement relates to the advice "Pap" Singleton gave to Blacks.
2. Report on the life and work of one of the Black inventors, scientists, doctors, or writers mentioned in this chapter.

# NEW VOICES OF PROTEST

Chapter 4

**AIM: What did Black leaders do to improve the conditions of Blacks in the early years of the twentieth century?**

1. In the early years of the twentieth century, new Black leaders appeared. They began to question Booker T. Washington's ideas. One of these leaders was W. E .B. Du Bois. Du Bois was the first Black to earn a Ph.D. degree from Harvard University. He was to become one of the most important Black leaders of the twentieth century. In 1903, Du Bois wrote a book called *The Soul of Black Folks*. He attacked Washington's policy of doing nothing about Jim Crow and the voting rights of Blacks. Du Bois also criticized Washington for not being interested in the education of bright young Blacks. He believed that Black progress depended on each young person, whom he called the "talented tenth." He said they should receive the best education possible so that they would be ready to be leaders.

2. In 1905, Du Bois called a meeting of Black professionals and thinkers at Niagara Falls. The purpose of the meeting was to work out new ways Blacks could best attack segregation and the other problems they faced. They called the group the **Niagara Movement.** The delegates declared, "We claim for ourselves every single right that belongs to a freeborn American, political, civil, and social; and until we get these rights we will never cease to protest." The Niagara Movement did not attract many Black supporters at first. It took the murder of eight Blacks near Abraham Lincoln's old home in Springfield, Illinois, in 1908, to convince many people that Washington's ideas did not work.

3. The next year, 1909, a group of Blacks and Whites decided that a new organization should be formed to fight for the rights of Blacks. Among them were a number of prominent women, both Black and White. Among the Black women were Ida Wells, the anti-lynching reformer, and Mary Church Terrell, a crusader for the rights of Blacks and women. The new organization was formed in 1910. It was called the National Association for the Advancement of Colored People **(NAACP).** In 1911, another important organization was formed. This was the **National Urban League.** Its purpose was to take care of the needs of Blacks in the growing cities.

4. W. E. B. Du Bois became editor of the magazine of the NAACP, *The Crisis*, and the organization's best-known leader as well. The NAACP won important cases it had brought before the Supreme Court. The court declared the grandfather clause was unconstitutional. It also ruled that a Black person could not be found guilty of murder if Blacks had been kept off the jury.

5. In spite of the efforts of Black organizations, conditions in the South were still bad. In 1910, Baltimore passed the first law that said that Blacks and Whites had to live in separate areas. Other southern cities soon copied this law. By 1915, the southern states had adopted "White **primary**" elections. Voters in primary elections choose candidates to run for public office. Only Whites could vote in the primaries of the Democratic party in the South. Because almost all elected officials in the South were Democrats, this system shut Blacks out of politics.

▲ W. E. B. Du Bois was a founder of the NAACP. For a quarter of a century he was its outspoken leader in the fight for the rights of Blacks.

A. Complete each sentence with one of the following names or terms.

W. E. B. Du Bois     White primary     National Association for
talented tenth      Niagara Movement     the Advancement of
The Crisis        The Soul of Black Folks    Colored People

1. _____ was the magazine of the NAACP.

2. _____ kept Blacks from taking part in Democratic party elections in the South.

3. W. E. B. Du Bois thought that the _____ of well-educated Blacks could become effective leaders.

4. _____ wrote that Blacks should actively work to regain their rights.

5. In his book called _____ , W. E. B. Du Bois attacked the views of Booker T. Washington.

6. A group of Black thinkers started the _____ to protest the treatment of Blacks.

7. Both Blacks and Whites began the _____ .

B. In each of the sentences that follow, the underlined word makes the sentence true or false. If the sentence is true, write **T** in the blank before it. If it is false, write the word or words that make it true.

_____ 1. W. E. B. Du Bois thought that Blacks should <u>accept</u> the Jim Crow system.

_____ 2. In southern states, Blacks were <u>unable</u> to vote in Primary elections.

_____ 3. Some southern cities passed laws <u>encouraging</u> Blacks to live in White neighborhoods.

_____ 4. The Supreme Court ruled that the grandfather clause was <u>unconstitutional</u>.

## Linking Past to Present

Study the time line. Then answer the questions.

1905
Black leaders meet
at Niagara Falls

1911
National Urban
League is formed

| 1900 | 1904 | 1908 | 1912 | 1916 | 1920 |

1903
W. E. B. Du Bois publishes
The Soul of Black Folks

1910
NAACP is
formed

1910
Baltimore passes
segregated
housing law

1915
Southern states adopt
"White primary"
elections

1. Two important Black organizations were founded in _____ and _____ .

2. Measures harmful to Blacks were passed in _____ and _____ .

3. The NAACP was formed _____ years after the meeting in Niagara Falls.

4. The NAACP is _____ years old in the year you are reading this book.

# Spotlight on People

**Matthew Henson.** On April 6, 1909, Matthew Henson became the first person to stand on the "top of the world," the North Pole. Henson, a Black, was a member of Robert Peary's expedition to the North Pole.

Seven earlier expeditions had failed before that April day. During 23 years of exploring in the Arctic region, Henson had learned the Eskimo language. He had mastered the skills needed to survive in the cold Arctic. Another member of the Peary expedition remembered: "He [Henson] was the most popular man aboard the ship with the Eskimos. He could talk their language like a native. He made all the sledges which went to the Pole. He made all the stoves. Henson, the colored man, went to the Pole with Peary because he was a better man than any of his [Peary's] White assistants."

Tragically, after the American flag had been planted on the North Pole, Peary refused to speak to Henson. No one knows for sure why this was so. Probably, Peary was angry that his assistant had reached the Pole first. For years he forbade Henson to lecture or show slides of their trip.

With his achievements little known, Henson had to work at jobs such as porter, carpenter, blacksmith, and messenger. However, after his death in 1955, the state of Maryland placed a plaque in his honor at the statehouse in Annapolis. This was the first time a Black had been so honored in the South. In 1988, The United States honored Henson. His remains were reburied in Arlington National Cemetery.

## Recalling the Facts

Choose each correct answer and write the letter in the space provided.

_____ 1. Matthew Henson was the first person
    a. to reach the North Pole.
    b. to reach the South Pole.
    c. to cross the Arctic Ocean.

_____ 2. The leader of the North Pole expedition was
    a. Matthew Henson.
    b. Robert Peary.
    c. an Eskimo.

_____ 3. Henson was popular with the Eskimos because
    a. he could stand the cold better than they could.
    b. he could speak their language.
    c. he lived in their houses.

_____ 4. A member of Peary's expedition said that
    a. Peary wanted a Black to have the honor of going to the Pole.
    b. Henson disliked the Eskimos.
    c. Henson was a better man than any of Peary's White assistants.

_____ 5. Probably Peary became angry with Henson because
    a. Henson would not follow Peary's orders.
    b. Henson reached the Pole before Peary.
    c. Henson caused the failure of the expedition.

# The Arts and Technology

**Ragtime.** At the end of the nineteenth century, a new style of music became the rage. It was called **ragtime.** It started in the Midwest, where it was popular in cafes and saloons. Black musicians spread the music to other areas of the country. Ragtime pianists set America's feet tapping. The music combined African rhythms with marching band music. It also drew from dances such as the polka and popular songs.

One of the most important ragtime musicians was Scott Joplin. Joplin started writing this new kind of music when he lived in Sedalia, Missouri. Many of the country's best pianists came to hear Joplin at Sedalia's Maple Leaf Club. In 1899, Joplin named his first "rag" song "The Maple Leaf Rag." When the song was published, it became an instant success. Another of Joplin's well-known rags is "The Entertainer," which he wrote in 1902. In 1973, it became the theme for the Oscar-winning movie *The Sting.*

Joplin spent years writing an opera in ragtime called *Treemonisha.* It was not appreciated at the time because rag's popularity had started to fade. It was finally performed in the 1970s. *Treemonisha* won the Pulitzer Prize for music in 1976, 57 years after its author's death.

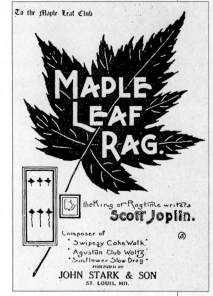

▲ One of Scott Joplin's most popular compositions was the "Maple Leaf Rag," which he composed in 1899.

1. What were the sources of ragtime music? _____

    _____

2. How did ragtime music become well known? _____

    _____

3. Why did it take so long for Joplin's opera to receive the Pulitzer Prize? _____

    _____

## CHAPTER REVIEW: CRITICAL THINKING

Late in his life, W. E. B. Du Bois described why his views differed from those of Booker T. Washington:

> He and I came from different backgrounds. I was born free. Washington was born a slave. I had a happy childhood and the acceptance of the community. Washington's childhood was hard. I had many more advantages: Fisk University, Harvard, graduate years in Europe. Washington had little formal schooling.

1. What reasons does DuBois suggest for the differences between his attitude and Washington's?

    _____

    _____

2. Explain how these differences would have made Washington believe Blacks should compromise. _____

    _____

    _____

# Chapter 5 WORLD WAR I

**AIM: What part did Blacks play in World War I? How well did they serve?**

1. W. E. B. Du Bois encouraged Blacks to back the Democratic candidate for president, Woodrow Wilson, in the election of 1912. This was a change for Blacks. They had long been loyal to the Republican party of Abraham Lincoln. Du Bois thought that Wilson would be sympathetic to the Black cause. However, after Wilson was elected, his policies turned out to be a disappointment. Wilson, a southerner, extended segregation to the federal government. In government offices, walls were put up to separate Black and White clerks. Dining and toilet facilities were also segregated. Blacks who had supported Wilson were outraged. They organized protests. A group of Blacks met with Wilson in the White House. Wilson told his visitors, "Segregation is not humiliating, but a benefit, and ought to be so regarded by you gentlemen."

▲ Black soldiers fought in many important battles in World War I. These soldiers are shown returning home after the war.

2. The United States entered World War I in 1917. President Wilson said the purpose of the war was to make the world safe for democracy. Blacks did not let their feelings about Wilson prevent them from supporting the war. However, they did ask why America should not also be made safe for democracy. Blacks had reason to raise this question. American armed forces discriminated against Blacks. Blacks who served in the army were commanded by Whites, even though the army had many Black officers.

3. One Black officer was Colonel Charles Young, a West Point graduate. He was the highest ranking Black officer. Young was forced to retire at the beginning of the war because he supposedly had high blood pressure. Young tried to show he was in good health by riding a horse 350 miles from Ohio to Washington, D.C. This did him no good. Blacks protested, and Young was finally allowed to serve in Europe four days before the war ended. Only after the NAACP and other Blacks complained did the army agree to train new Black officers.

4. About 300,000 Blacks took part in World War I. Half of them served in France, mostly unloading ships and moving supplies. When Blacks did get a chance to fight, they served bravely. Black troops usually fought under French officers and took part in many of the war's important battles. One Black regiment held out for 191 days against German attacks without losing ground.

5. The Germans spread leaflets telling Blacks they were foolish to fight for a White-ruled country. Yet not a single Black American deserted. Black troops were the first American soldiers to cross the Rhine River into Germany. Two Black soldiers, Henry Johnson and Needham Roberts, received the French military medal for bravery in action. General John Pershing, the American commander, told a Black unit, "The American public has every reason to be proud of your record."

## Understanding What You Have Read

**A.** Write the name of the person next to the statement he might have made.

Gen. John Pershing    Woodrow Wilson    Col. Charles Young    Needham Roberts

_____ 1. I was a Black officer who was not allowed to serve in World War I until near the end.

_____ 2. I received the French medal for bravery in battle.

_____ 3. I was the president who told a group of Blacks that segregation was a benefit.

_____ 4. I told the Black troops that they had every reason to be proud of their record.

**B.** In each of the sentences that follow, the underlined word makes the sentence true or false. If the sentence is true, write **T** in the blank before it. If it is false, write the word or words that make the sentence true.

_____ 1. Black support for Woodrow Wilson was unusual because Wilson was a <u>Republican</u>.

_____ 2. Black soldiers in World War I were <u>not</u> allowed to serve in White units.

_____ 3. The Germans <u>successfully</u> tried to persuade Black soldiers to desert from the U.S. army.

_____ 4. Black troops fought in <u>some</u> important battles of World War I.

_____ 5. <u>Most</u> Black troops in Europe did labor such as moving supplies.

## Daily Life

**The Home Front.** On the home front, Blacks supported the war in many ways. They bought over $250 million worth of war bonds and stamps. They worked in ammunition factories. They produced food and cooperated in the wartime drive not to waste food. Yet conditions were no better for Blacks than they had been before the war.

Everyday life in Washington, D.C., was difficult for Blacks. Many had come from the South in the hope of getting work in the nation's capital. Black neighborhoods became more crowded. Streetcars and schools were segregated. Blacks were not allowed into the downtown hotels and restaurants. At theaters, Blacks had to sit in the "colored gallery," usually a shabby balcony.

▲ Blacks helped build America's armed might in World War I. These men are working in a shipyard.

How did Blacks support the war? _____

_____

# Spotlight on People

**Mary Church Terrell.** Mary Church Terrell was a Black teacher in Washington, D.C. During the war, she volunteered for a government job. On the application form, she wrote "American" in answer to the question asking for her race. By mistake, she was assigned to a Whites-only office. When the mistake was discovered, she was ordered to an all-Black department. She resigned in protest.

Terrell devoted her long life to fighting injustice. Born in 1863, she herself had grown up with many advantages. Her father was the South's first Black millionaire. She attended Oberlin College, which had been accepting Blacks since 1835. After college, her father wanted her to return home to the comfortable life of her family. However, she was determined to find useful work.

Friends had warned her that she would never marry because no Black man would be as well-educated as she was. However, in Washington, D.C., she met her future husband, Robert H. Terrell, a Harvard graduate. He became one of the country's few Black judges.

As with Ida Wells, the lynching of a close friend turned Mary Terrell into a crusader. She helped set up the National Association of Colored Women in 1896. She was one of the first members of the NAACP. Her ability as a speaker made her a popular lecturer. She was tireless in telling people about the injustices that American Blacks faced.

Terrell also joined the fight to get women the right to vote. At age 87, she led a group demanding the right of Blacks to eat in Washington restaurants. She inspired others by marching for hours with a cane in one hand and a picket sign in the other. When she died in 1954, her body lay in state at the new Washington headquarters of the NAACP. Thousands passed by, paying tribute to this remarkable woman.

## Recalling the Facts

Choose each correct answer and write the letter in the space provided.

_____ 1. As a child, Mary Church
    a. experienced great hardship.
    b. lived in a ghetto.
    c. had many advantages.

_____ 2. Terrell's father did not want her
    a. to get an education.
    b. to marry.
    c. to work.

_____ 3. Terrell resigned from her government job because
    a. she did not have to earn a living.
    b. her father died.
    c. she refused to work in a segregated office.

_____ 4. Terrell's speaking ability
    a. did not come easily to her.
    b. made her a popular lecturer.
    c. was seldom used.

_____ 5. In her old age, Mary Church Terrell
    a. continued working as hard as ever.
    b. felt that she had been a failure.
    c. was almost forgotten.

# The Arts and Technology

**Invention.** Garrett A. Morgan was a Black inventor who was responsible for an invention we are aware of every day of our lives—the traffic light. Morgan was born in Paris, Tennessee, in 1875. Little is known about his early life. Like Thomas A. Edison and Henry Ford, he was one of those self-taught inventors who learn best through reading and experimenting.

In 1901, Morgan invented a belt that enabled sewing machines to fasten buttons on clothes. He sold it for $150. In the years that followed, he worked on a helmet to protect miners and fire fighters from smoke and gas. In 1914, he entered his invention in a contest sponsored by the International Exposition of Sanitation and Safety. It won the First Grand Prize gold medal.

In 1916, Morgan showed how his helmet could be put to good use. There was an explosion at the waterworks in Cleveland, Ohio. Many workers were trapped in a tunnel below Lake Erie. Rescuers could not reach them because of fumes in the tunnel. Morgan arrived with a number of his helmets. The rescuers put them on and were able to reach the trapped workers and save them.

Morgan continued to apply his imagination to solving problems. In the early twentieth century, automobiles were becoming

▲ Garrett A. Morgan is shown here with an exhibit of some of his inventions, including the traffic light.

the most popular form of transportation in the United States. However, cities were becoming clogged with traffic. Also, there were many accidents. It was not possible to put a police officer at every corner where roads crossed.

Morgan thought up the idea of having a light at each corner that told oncoming cars to stop or go. He invented a timer that would automatically change the light. Cities around the country soon wanted Morgan's traffic lights. He could not make enough of them to meet the demand. He sold the rights to his invention to the General Electric Company. He was paid $40,000, a huge amount for the time. Everybody who stops at a red light today is using Morgan's idea.

1. Morgan's first invention enabled sewing machines _____

2. Morgan's helmet helped to save _____

_____

3. Morgan's invention that is used every day is _____

# CHAPTER REVIEW: CRITICAL THINKING

Why do you think Blacks usually supported Lincoln's Republican Party? _____

_____

_____

2. If you were a Black in 1917, how would you have reacted when President Wilson said the world had to be made safe for democracy? _____

_____

# THE GREAT MigrATion

Chapter **6**

1. Since Reconstruction, southern Blacks had been leaving the rural areas. Many went to the North and the West. Around 1915, the pace of this movement quickened. From 1915 to 1925, over one million Blacks left the South and settled in such cities as Chicago, St. Louis, Detroit, and New York. Smaller numbers went to the West Coast. This movement of Black Americans is known as the **Great Migration.**

2. There were many reasons for the migration. Better job opportunities were one reason. In 1915, the Ku Klux Klan was revived. Southern Blacks moved North to escape lynchings and racial hatred. The next year, an insect, the **boll weevil,** destroyed much of the cotton crop. Black farmers left their land to seek work elsewhere. Another reason for the migration was the war in Europe. It cut off the flow of immigrants to the United States. This resulted in greater job opportunities for Blacks. After the war, growing industries such as automobile manufacturing created new jobs. By 1926, the Ford Company was employing more than 10,000 Blacks.

3. Blacks found that they faced almost as much prejudice against them in the North. The newcomers were forced to live in parts of cities that became Black ghettoes. A **ghetto** is a place where people of a certain group are forced to live. These ghettoes, such as Harlem in New York City and the South Side of Chicago, were more crowded than other parts of the city. Overcrowded housing was one of the causes of riots in Chicago in 1919. Whites in the northern cities often resented the newcomers who competed with them for jobs. Unions discriminated against Blacks, making it difficult for them to get jobs in many trades. Overcrowding and unemployment made the ghettoes breeding grounds for crime and other social problems.

4. Still, opportunities were greater in the North than in the South. The National Urban League helped migrants find jobs and adjust to city life. At least, in the North, Blacks could vote. Their increasing numbers made them a force in elections. The migration produced new Black leaders. In Chicago, Oscar DePriest was elected city councilman in 1916. A Republican, he became the first Black representative from Chicago in 1928.

5. One of the most important Black leaders of the 1920s was Marcus Garvey. Born in Jamaica, he came to New York in 1916. He formed the Universal Negro Improvement Association **(UNIA).** Garvey said Blacks should control their own economic future. He urged Blacks to get ready to return to their homeland in Africa. He published a newspaper, the *Negro World.* In it he preached that Blacks were a gifted people with a proud past and a great future. Garvey's "Back to Africa" message met with an enthusiastic response from Blacks. In a few years, Garvey claimed more than two million followers. Garvey's movement collapsed in 1923, however, when he was convicted of mail fraud and sentenced to prison.

▲ Marcus Garvey believed Black Americans should move to Africa. He said they would never receive equal treatment in the United States.

# Understanding What You Have Read

A. Match the cause in the left-hand column with its effect in the right-hand column.

_____ 1. The boll weevil

_____ 2. World War I

_____ 3. The revival of the Ku Klux Klan

_____ 4. Overcrowded housing in ghettoes

_____ 5. Blacks' ability to vote in the North

a. caused Chicago riots of 1919.

b. gave Blacks political power.

c. cut off the flow of immigrants to the U.S.

d. caused the failure of the southern cotton crop.

e. increased lynchings and racial hatred.

B. Fill in the blank in each sentence with the correct name or term below.

Oscar DePriest    Marcus Garvey    National Urban League
Great Migration    Ford Company    *The Negro World*

1. The _____ was a mass movement of Blacks from 1915 to 1925.

2. The _____ employed more than 10,000 Blacks in 1926.

3. _____ was a Black Republican congressman from Chicago.

4. _____ preached a message of "Back to Africa."

5. _____ was Marcus Garvey's newspaper.

6. The _____ helped Blacks find jobs and adjust to city life.

# Building Geography Skills

Study the map. Then answer the questions.

1. The region from which the Blacks migrated was located in the _____.

2. Blacks migrated to _____ cities located east of the Mississippi River than west of the river.

3. The principal destinations in the Great Lakes area were the industrial cities of _____

_____.

4. Blacks migrating northeastward headed for the cities of

_____

_____.

**The Great Migration**

The Great Lakes area

Cleveland

Detroit

Chicago

Oakland

San Francisco

Los Angeles

St. Louis

Cincinatti
Louisville

New York
Philadelphia
Baltimore
Washington, D.C.

New Orleans

- More than 30% Black in 1920
- Migration routes
- Principal destinations

0    400  Miles

0    400  Kilometers

# Spotlight on People

**Robert S. Abbott.** One of the most important voices urging Blacks to move north was Robert S. Abbott. Abbott was born in Georgia in 1870. His father had been a slave. Abbott went to colleges in the South. He moved to Chicago. There, in 1905, he founded the *Chicago Defender*. Gradually, he build the *Defender* into the most important Black newspaper of its time. He used bold headlines and printed stories about ordinary people. Abbott became a powerful force in Chicago politics. The governor of Illinois named him to the state Race Relations Commission after the riots of 1919.

In his newspaper, Abbott attacked discrimination, segregation, and lynching. He hired such able writers as Ida Wells. In the *Defender*, she reported on the East St. Louis riots. The poetry of Gwendolyn Brooks, a leading Black writer, first appeared in Abbott's paper. He built the circulation of the *Defender* to 200,000 copies weekly. The newspaper was mailed out of Chicago to Blacks all over the United States. In the South, it was passed from hand to hand. In every issue, Abbott urged southern Blacks to come North. The paper gave advice to the migrants. It published a 26-point "guide to conduct." One of its warnings was: "Keep your mouth shut, please! There is entirely too much talking on the streetcars among our newcomers."

Abbott was hopeful about the future of race relations. In a 1915 editorial, he wrote, "Slowly but surely all over this country we are gradually edging in from this place and then that place, getting a foothold before making a place for our brother. By this only can the so-called race problem be solved. It is merely a question of a better and a closer understanding between the races. We are Americans and must live together, so why not live in peace?"

## Recalling the Facts

Choose each correct answer and write the letter in the space provided.

_____ 1. Robert Abbott was the son of
    **a.** a former slave.
    **b.** a wealthy manufacturer.
    **c.** a newspaper reporter.

_____ 2. One reason Abbott's newspaper was popular was that
    **a.** it appealed to white audiences.
    **b.** it printed news about sports.
    **c.** it had stories about ordinary people.

_____ 3. Abbott was powerful in
    **a.** Southern politics.
    **b.** Washington, D.C., politics.
    **c.** Chicago politics.

_____ 4. The *Chicago Defender* was read
    **a.** only in Chicago.
    **b.** in many areas of the country.
    **c.** by a few educated people.

_____ 5. Abbott felt that race relations
    **a.** would improve.
    **b.** would get worse.
    **c.** would always remain the same.

_____ 6. Abbott felt that the race problem would be solved when
    **a.** Blacks had moved to Africa.
    **b.** Blacks fought the system by force.
    **c.** there was better and closer understanding between the races.

# The Arts and Technology

**Jazz.** Moving North with the Great Migration was the music called **jazz**. Jazz arose among Blacks in New Orleans. A decade after the Civil War, jazz bands paraded in New Orleans. The music was not written down. The great jazz musicians improvised, or made up the music as they played. They took a tune and wove musical patterns from it. Musicians on riverboats spread jazz up the Mississippi River.

One of the early jazz musicians was Ferdinand "Jelly Roll" Morton. He left New Orleans in the early 1900s. Traveling to cities in the North and South, he made fans for the music. Jazz got another boost when Joseph "King" Oliver left New Orleans in 1917. His Creole Jazz Band became a big hit in Chicago. In 1922, he added Louis Armstrong to his band. The two had met in New Orleans when Armstrong was delivering coal in the daytime and playing his trumpet at night. Armstrong became the most popular jazz trumpeter in history.

The popularity of jazz spread throughout the country and Europe. Phonograph records—a recent invention—let many

▲ This is King Oliver's band in Chicago in 1923. Oliver is standing behind Lil Hardin, the pianist. Louis Armstrong is to Oliver's right.

more people hear the new music. Armstrong started his own band, the Louis Armstrong Hot Five. They made many outstanding records. Many White musicians also organized jazz bands. Jazz became so popular among Whites, as well as Blacks, that the era of the 1920s is often called "The Jazz Age."

1. What was the connection between the Great Migration and the spread of jazz music?

_____

_____

2. How did the phonograph record affect the popularity of jazz? _____

_____

## CHAPTER REVIEW: CRITICAL THINKING

1. Blacks like Marcus Garvey felt that Blacks could only be truly free in a country of their own. Why was this message so popular with many Blacks in the United States in the 1920s?

_____

_____

2. Some Blacks, such as W. E. B. Du Bois and Robert Abbott, opposed Garvey's views. What gave these Black leaders reason to hope that conditions for Blacks in the United States would improve? _____

_____

# Chapter 7 THE BLACK RENAISSANCE

**AIM: What was the Black Renaissance? Who took part in it?**

1. In the 1920s, Harlem, a section of New York City where mostly Blacks lived, became the cultural capital of Black America. Many talented young Black writers, actors, and entertainers lived and worked there. They were part of what is known as the Black, or Harlem, Renaissance. The word **renaissance** means "rebirth." The **Black Renaissance** of the 1920s was a flowering of Black American art and thought.

2. The poet Langston Hughes, who was born in Cleveland, Ohio, came to Harlem because he believed it was the "greatest Negro city in the world." In Harlem, Hughes met other Black writers. Among them were Claude McKay, Countee Cullen, Arna Bontemps, and Jean Toomer. Among the women writers of the Harlem Renaissance were Jessie Fauset and Georgia Douglas Johnson. The writers found a

▲ Langston Hughes was one of the most talented poets of the Black Renaissance.

patron, or supporter, in A'Lelia Walker, daughter of Madame C. J. Walker. The Walker mansion, known as the Dark Tower, was a meeting place for young writers and thinkers. Soon their work drew the attention of the country at large. In 1926, Hughes stated the goal of the Black Renaissance: "We younger Negro artists who create now intend to express our individual dark-skinned selves without fear or shame."

3. An older member of the Black Renaissance was James Weldon Johnson. With his brother, J. Rosamund Johnson, he wrote the song "Lift Every Voice and Sing." It is sometimes called the Black national anthem.

4. Historian Arthur Schomburg came to the United States from Puerto Rico. In 1911 he helped to start the Negro Society for Historical Research. He is best remembered today for his vast collection of works on Afro-America history. This collection is now housed in its own building in Harlem. Another historian, Carter Woodson, is known as the father of Negro history. In 1916, he began the *Journal of Negro History*. It has been important in helping to discover the history of Afro-Americans. Woodson is the originator of Black History Week. Zorah Neal Hurston was a Black anthropologist who wrote about the folklore of Haiti and Jamaica. She is also remembered for her novels and short stories.

5. In the 1920s, many Black actors appeared in the New York theater in plays written by Whites. In 1920, the Black actor Charles Gilpin played the title role in Eugene O'Neill's *The Emperor Jones*. Later Paul Robeson appeared in another play by O'Neill. He also acted in the movie of *The Emperor Jones*. Robeson was the country's best-known Black actor for 30 years. He was also a great singer. The actress Rose McClendon performed in the play *Porgy* in 1927. This play was later made into an opera by George Gershwin called *Porgy and Bess*. In 1921, the first Broadway play written and acted by Blacks appeared. It was called *Shuffle Along*.

**A.** Write the name of the person next to the statement he or she might have made.

A'Lelia Walker     James Weldon Johnson     Zorah Neal Hurston
Arthur Schomburg     Carter Woodson     Paul Robeson

_____ **1.** I made a collection of books and manuscripts of Afro-American history.

_____ **2.** I was the best-known Black actor and singer for 30 years.

_____ **3.** I was co-author of the song "Lift Every Voice and Sing."

_____ **4.** Members of the Black Renaissance met in my mansion.

_____ **5.** I started Black History Week.

_____ **6.** I wrote about the folklore of Haiti and Jamaica.

**B.** Match the name or term in the left-hand column with the description of it in the right-hand column.

_____ **1.** Harlem

**a.** A flowering of Black art and thought that reached its peak in the 1920s

_____ **2.** Black Renaissance

**b.** the first Broadway play written and acted by Blacks

_____ **3.** *Shuffle Along*

**c.** a part of New York City that became the cultural capital of Black America in the 1920s

_____ **4.** the Dark Tower

**d.** a magazine that has published important articles on Afro-American history

_____ **5.** *Journal of Negro History*

**e.** meeting place for members of the Black Renaissance

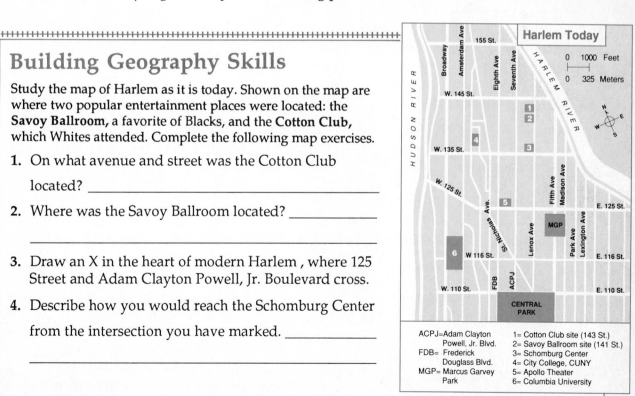

# Building Geography Skills

Study the map of Harlem as it is today. Shown on the map are where two popular entertainment places were located: the **Savoy Ballroom,** a favorite of Blacks, and the **Cotton Club,** which Whites attended. Complete the following map exercises.

1. On what avenue and street was the Cotton Club located? _____

2. Where was the Savoy Ballroom located? _____

_____

3. Draw an X in the heart of modern Harlem , where 125 Street and Adam Clayton Powell, Jr. Boulevard cross.

4. Describe how you would reach the Schomburg Center from the intersection you have marked. _____

_____

**Harlem Today**

0   1000   Feet
0   325   Meters

HUDSON RIVER
HARLEM RIVER

Broadway
Amsterdam Ave
Eighth Ave
Seventh Ave

155 St.
W. 145 St.
W. 135 St.
W. 125 St.
W. 116 St.
W. 110 St.

St. Nicholas Ave.
Lenox Ave
Fifth Ave
Madison Ave
Park Ave
Lexington Ave

E. 125 St.
E. 116 St.
E. 110 St.

MGP

CENTRAL PARK

FDB
ACPJ

ACPJ= Adam Clayton Powell, Jr. Blvd.
FDB= Frederick Douglass Blvd.
MGP= Marcus Garvey Park

1= Cotton Club site (143 St.)
2= Savoy Ballroom site (141 St.)
3= Schomburg Center
4= City College, CUNY
5= Apollo Theater
6= Columbia University

# Spotlight on People

▲ Duke Ellington was one of the most popular jazz band leaders and composers. He started his band in the 1920s and continued to perform with it for more than forty years.

**Cotton Club Headliners.** White New Yorkers often went "uptown" to Harlem for entertainment. The most famous place they went was the Cotton Club. The greatest Black musicians, dancers, and singers appeared there. However, the entertainers were the only Blacks allowed in.

The Cotton Club opened in 1927. One of the first bands to appear there was that of Edward Kennedy "Duke" Ellington. Duke Ellington was born in Washington, D.C., in 1899. He started his first jazz band there as a teenager. Ellington became famous from his appearances at the Cotton Club and became one of the greatest musicians in the history of jazz. Other jazz greats who performed at the Cotton Club included Cab Calloway and Lionel Hampton.

One of the dancers who appeared in the Cotton Club's colorful floor shows was the young Lena Horne. She went on to become one of the best-known singers of popular music. She sang with Black and White bands and also appeared in the movies.

A Cotton Club favorite was the tap dancer Bill "Bojangles" Robinson. Many people believe he was the greatest of all tap dancers. One of his specialties was tap dancing up and down a staircase.

Ethel Waters started her career as a singer at the Cotton Club and later became a great dramatic actress. She appeared in Broadway musicals and plays. She helped to popularize the song "Stormy Weather."

The Cotton Club moved out of Harlem in the late 1930s. However, its popularity did not follow it elsewhere.

## Recalling the Facts

Choose each correct answer and write the letter in the space provided.

_____ 1. The customers of the Cotton Club were
    a. only Blacks.
    b. only Whites.
    c. both Blacks and Whites.

_____ 2. Entertainment at the Cotton Club included
    a. musicians only.
    b. dancers and singers.
    c. bands, dancers, and singers.

_____ 3. Bill "Bojangles" Robinson was a
    a. great tap dancer.
    b. band leader.
    c. singer.

_____ 4. Performers who sang at the Cotton Club included
    a. Ethel Waters and Lena Horne.
    b. Ethel Waters.
    c. Ethel Waters and Lionel Hampton.

_____ 5. The band leader who became famous from his appearances at the Cotton Club was
    a. Duke Ellington.
    b. Cab Calloway.
    c. Benny Goodman.

# Using Primary Sources

No poet did more to tell the world how it felt to be Black than Langston Hughes. Here are two of his poems.

## Words Like Freedom

There are words like *Freedom*
Sweet and wonderful to say.
On my heartstrings freedom sings
All day everyday.

There are words like *Liberty*
That almost make me cry.
If you had known what I know
You would know why.

## Dream Variations

To fling my arms wide
In some place of the sun,
To whirl and to dance
Till the white day is done.
Then rest at cool evening
Beneath a tall tree
While night comes on gently,
    Dark like me—
That is my dream!

To fling my arms wide
In the face of the sun,
Dance! Whirl! Whirl!
Till the quick day is done.
Rest at pale evening . . .
A tall, slim tree . . .
Night coming tenderly
    Black like me.

1. In the poem "Words Like Freedom," what does the poet mean by the last two lines?

   _____

   _____

2. In "Dream Variations," Hughes contrasts day and night. What does he associate with

   each? _____

   _____

## CHAPTER REVIEW: CRITICAL THINKING

1. Why did Harlem become the center of Black thought and culture? Give your reasons.

   _____

   _____

2. What effect do you think the Black Renaissance had on Whites' attitudes toward Blacks?

   _____

   _____

# UNIT 2 REVIEW

## Summary of the Unit

A few of the most important events and facts presented in Unit 2 are listed below. Write these events and facts in your notebook and and add three more.

1. The National Association for the Advancement of Colored People (NAACP) was formed to fight segregation and discrimination against Black Americans.
2. Blacks served in segregated army units in World War I. They fought bravely and earned respect for their ability.
3. Between 1915 and 1925, more than a million Blacks left the South to settle elsewhere. This movement was called the Great Migration.
4. In the 1920s, Black writers and thinkers produced many fine works. This flowering of culture was known as the Black Renaissance.

## Understanding What You Have Read

Choose each correct answer and write the letter in the space provided.

_____ 1. Both the Niagara Movement and the National Association for the Advancement of Colored People (NAACP) wanted
    a. to help Blacks gain their rights as citizens.
    b. to show that Blacks accepted the Jim Crow system.
    c. to persuade Blacks to be content with their lives.

_____ 2. W. E. B. Du Bois
    a. agreed with the views of Booker T. Washington.
    b. disagreed with the views of Booker T. Washington.
    c. told Blacks to move to Africa.

_____ 3. After some Blacks supported Woodrow Wilson in the election of 1912,
    a. Wilson urged Congress to help Blacks.
    b. Wilson overturned the Jim Crow laws.
    c. Wilson disappointed them by supporting segregation.

_____ 4. In World War I, Blacks
    a. fought in integrated units with White soldiers.
    b. fought in segregated units.
    c. saw no action in battles.

_____ 5. When Blacks moved out of the South in the Great Migration,
    a. they were helped by the federal government.
    b. they found prejudice in other places.
    c. they soon returned.

_____ 6. The Black Renaissance reached its peak
    a. in the 1800s.
    b. between 1900 and 1910.
    c. in the 1920s.

## Building Your Vocabulary

Complete each of the following sentences by using one of the words that follow.

boll weevil    ghetto    renaissance    race riot
primary    expedition    migration

_____ 1. A _____ is a neighborhood where members of one racial or religious group are forced to live.

_____ 2. The _____ was an insect that attacked the South's cotton crop.

_____ 3. A _____ is an election that chooses candidates to run for public office.

_____ 4. Public violence that results from conflict between the races is called a _____.

_____ 5. A trip made to explore or find a new place is called an _____.

_____ 6. A mass movement of people is called a _____.

_____ 7. A rebirth of culture and thought is often called a _____.

## Developing Ideas and Skills—Using Graphs

Study the graph below. Then decide whether or not each statement is true. If the statement is true, write **T** next to it. If it is false, write **F**. Then rewrite the statement to make it true.

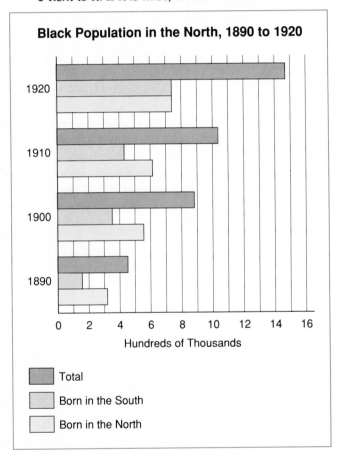

**Black Population in the North, 1890 to 1920**

Hundreds of Thousands

Total
Born in the South
Born in the North

_____ 1. In 1900, the total Black population of the North was over 1,000,000.

_____
_____

_____ 2. In 1920, the total Black population of the North was over 1,400,000.

_____
_____

_____ 3. In 1900, the Black population of the North included as many Blacks born in the South as Blacks born elsewhere.

_____
_____
_____

_____ 4. In 1920, the number of Blacks in the North who were born in the South was over 1,000,000.

_____
_____
_____

## Making History Live

1. Read more of the poetry of Langston Hughes, Countee Cullen, or Jessie Fauset. Tell why their poems are important to you.
2. Prepare oral reports on ragtime and jazz musicians discussed in this unit. Listen to some of the recordings of this music and explain why you think it made history.
3. Role-play one of the individuals discussed in the unit. Explain how your work will help gain equality for Blacks.

# THE GREAT DEPRESSION

Chapter **8**

1. In October 1929, prices on the New York Stock Exchange tumbled. Before long the country found itself in the grip of the **Great Depression.** A **depression** is a time of severe economic hardship. Thousands of banks and businesses closed. Millions of people lost their jobs. A feeling of hopelessness spread across the land. Blacks were among those hardest hit by the depression. In 1930, more than half the Blacks in northern cities had lost their jobs. Relief payments from the government helped both the Blacks and the Whites who were jobless.

2. Blacks tried to cope with the hard times any way they could. One way was to hold **"rent parties."** People charged admission to parties in their own apartments to pay the rent. Black churches opened free "soup kitchens" to feed the hungry. In some cities, people joined together to buy food in large quantities to get lower prices.

3. Farmers in the South suffered as well as city people. The costs of farming went up while the prices farmers received for their crops went down. This squeeze forced many small farmers out of business. Black farmers by the thousands left the land they had worked for generations. Many of them came north to the already crowded cities, where there were soup and bread lines for the jobless.

4. In the 1930s, a movement was organized in the Harlem section of New York City that tried to help Blacks through the difficult times. This was the Father Divine Peace Mission Movement. Father Divine was a Black leader whose original name was George Baker. Divine stressed peace and harmony between the races, and his movement was open to all races. He opened restaurants that gave away food to thousands of poor Blacks. His followers did not accept government **welfare.** Instead they opened many small businesses. The movement spread to other cities during the depression.

5. Joining a labor union was one way workers during the Great Depression tried to protect their jobs, improve their working conditions, and increase their wages. A **labor union** is an organization that fights for workers' rights. One of the first successful unions with Black members was the Brotherhood of Sleeping Car Porters. It was organized by A. Philip Randolph in 1925. In the 1930s, a new union group, called the Congress of Industrial Organizations **(CIO),** was formed. It reached out to both Black and White workers in the automobile industry, mining, and other industries. By the end of the 1930s, over 200,000 Black workers were in CIO unions. This was only a small part of the Black labor force, but Blacks were making progress in fighting for their rights as workers.

6. In 1932, the voters elected Franklin D. Roosevelt president. He started programs that were aimed at bringing the United States out of the Great Depression and helping Americans who suffered from the effects of the depression.

▲ The Great Depression left many Black workers without jobs. What is the worker in this picture doing?

## Understanding What You Have Read

**A.** Write the term or name that best fits each sentence in the space provided.

labor union        Father Divine    CIO
A. Philip Randolph    depression

1. A _____ is a time of severe economic hardship.

2. A _____ is an organization that fights for workers' rights.

3. The Brotherhood of Sleeping Car Porters was started by _____.

4. _____ started a movement that called for racial harmony.

5. The _____ was a union group that reached out to both Blacks and Whites.

**B.** In each of the sentences that follow, the underlined word makes the sentence true or false. If the sentence is true, write **T** in the blank before it. If it is false, write the word or words that make it true.

_____ 1. The Great Depression hurt <u>both</u> Blacks and Whites.

_____ 2. During the depression, the price of farm products <u>rose</u>.

_____ 3. To help pay their rent, people charged admission to <u>movies</u> in their homes.

_____ 4. To get lower prices, Blacks joined together in buying <u>food</u>.

## Daily Life

**Detroit in the Great Depression.** Detroit was one city that was especially hard hit by the Great Depression. Henry Ford's wages of $5 a day had drawn many Blacks from the South in the 1920s. When the depression hit, Ford and other auto makers in the "Motor City" had to lay off workers. In the worst years of the depression (1931–1933), auto workers earned 76 cents an hour. Those who had jobs felt lucky.

The depression spread to all aspects of life in Detroit, not just jobs. Poverty put strains on Black families as fathers, mothers, and children struggled to stay alive.

During the 1930s, the United Auto Workers (UAW) union fought a long battle to get the workers in the automobile industry to join the union. Some Blacks sided with the

▲ These workers are making engine blocks in one of Detroit's auto factories.

Ford company and did not join the UAW. They felt loyalty to Ford for giving them jobs when others would not. Finally, most Black workers did join the UAW.

1. The auto industry _____ workers during the Great Depression.

2. Some Blacks did not join the UAW because _____
_____.

# Spotlight on People

**Billie Holiday.** Billie Holiday was one of the most popular singers of her day. She had an individual singing style that combined blues and jazz to produce an unforgettable sound. When she sang of sorrow and pain, she drew heavily on her own experience.

Holiday was born Eleanora Fagan in Baltimore, Maryland, in 1915. Not long after she was born, her father, a guitar player, left the family. As a child, she was in and out of reform schools. People called her "Bill" because they thought she was as rough as a boy. Later, when she became a singer, she took the name "Billie Holiday."

Holiday and her mother moved to New York when she was 13. About that time, she heard the records of Bessie Smith and Louis Armstrong. Both performers were to have a strong influence on Holiday's singing style.

During the depression years, Holiday went to a Harlem night club and asked the owner for a job. As she recalled, "I told him I could sing. He said, '*Sing*.'" When she did, "The customers stopped drinking. They turned around and watched." The owner hired her.

Benny Goodman, the famous band leader and clarinet player, hired Holiday to sing with his band. Then she began to sing with Artie Shaw's jazz band. They called her "Lady Day" because of her dignified manners. Shaw and most of his band were White. In one city, a restaurant refused to serve Holiday. One of the band members said, "This is Lady Day. Now you feed her."

Holiday still faced prejudice. Shaw's band was given a radio show. The producers cut back on Holiday's appearances. They felt listeners in the South would object to a Black singer performing with a White band.

Holiday's later years were difficult, and she died at the age of 44. She is remembered as one of the great singers of popular music. Each year thousands of copies of her records are bought.

## Recalling the Facts

Choose each correct answer and write the letter in the space provided.

_____ 1. Billie Holiday's singing style was a blend of
    a. jazz and rock.
    b. blues and jazz.
    c. spirituals and jazz.

_____ 2. Her singing style was influenced by
    a. Louis Armstrong and Bessie Smith.
    b. Benny Goodman.
    c. Artie Shaw.

_____ 3. She got the nickname "Lady Day" because
    a. she had dignified manners.
    b. she liked to sing in the daytime.
    c. she pretended to be British.

_____ 4. As a Black singer with a White band, Billie Holiday
    a. was not accepted by the band members.
    b. was accepted by white restaurants.
    c. faced prejudice.

# The Arts and Technology

**The Blues.** The blues have been part of Black American music since the 1800s. At first the blues told about the sorrows of life in the South. After the Great Migration, many blues songs dealt with the loneliness and confusion of living in the cities. William C. Handy was one of the first to write down blues music. His "St. Louis Blues" of 1914 is one of the best-known American songs. In the 1920s, the blues became more popular through the singing of Gertrude (Ma) Rainey.

The most popular blues singer was Bessie Smith. Bessie Smith was born in Chattanooga, Tennessee, in 1894. She got her start as a singer while touring with Ma Rainey. Through her recordings, Smith became known to millions. Her record of "Down Hearted Blues" sold two million copies in one year. The power and beauty of her voice and the songs she sang earned Bessie Smith the title "Empress of the Blues." Her fame grew after her death in 1937. Some critics regard Bessie Smith as the greatest of all jazz artists.

▲ In the 1920s and 1930s, Bessie Smith was the most popular singer of the blues.

1. How did the Great Migration change the subject of blues music? _____

    _____

2. How do you know that Bessie Smith was a popular singer? _____

    _____

## CHAPTER REVIEW: CRITICAL THINKING

The Great Depression affected all Americans. People lost their jobs, many went hungry, and thousands became homeless.

1.  People and groups responded differently to the depression. Compare the actions taken by the following in dealing with the depression: Black churches, Black farmers in the South,

    followers of Father Divine, Black automobile workers. _____

    _____

    _____

2.  If you had been a labor leader during the depression, what arguments would you have used

    to persuade workers to join your union? _____

    _____

    _____

# 9 THE NEW DEAL

1. When Franklin D. Roosevelt became president in 1933, he resolved to do many things to help the country deal with the Great Depression. Roosevelt wanted the United States government to do everything possible to help the millions of Americans who were hurt by the depression. The programs he started are known as the **New Deal.** With the New Deal, the government for the first time took on the responsibility of helping all Americans in need.

2. The New Deal programs aided hundreds of thousands of Black and White Americans. Needy persons of all races received relief in the form of cash payments. The Civilian Conservation Corps (CCC) hired hundreds of thousands of Black and White young men to plant trees, build dams, and reclaim forest lands. The Farm Security Administration (FSA) helped 50,000 Black farmers move to better land. Black workers in the Public Works Administration (PWA) helped build bridges and roads, schools, playgrounds, community centers, and other public facilities.

3. The largest federal relief agency of the New Deal was the Works Progress Administration (WPA). The WPA gave jobs to more than one million Blacks. This was more than any other New Deal agency. WPA workers were employed as clerks, teachers, and other professionals. The WPA gave jobs to many Black writers, including Claude McKay, Richard Wright, and Ralph Ellison, and artists, including painter Jacob Lawrence and sculptor Selma Burke. WPA programs also employed Black playwrights and actors.

4. President Roosevelt sought the advice of many Black leaders. He had an informal group of Black leaders who were known as the Black Cabinet. One well-known member of the Black Cabinet was Mary McLeod Bethune. Bethune became the first Black woman to head a federal office, the Negro Affairs Division of the National Youth Administration (NYA).

5. Eleanor Roosevelt, the president's wife, took a particular interest in the problems of Blacks. She often visited Black institutions and areas where Blacks lived. She consulted with Black leaders and supported civil rights even before the term was in general use. She counted Mary McLeod Bethune as a political colleague and friend. Her interest in the rights of all people continued to grow, and her influence in support of Blacks persisted until her death.

6. President Roosevelt was a Democrat. His policies helped change the longtime loyalty of Blacks to the Republican Party. Blacks viewed Roosevelt as a president who was very much interested in the conditions of Blacks. In 1936, a majority of Blacks voted Democratic for the first time. In every presidential election since then, most Blacks have backed the Democratic candidate. The New Deal was truly a turning point in the history of the United States and in the lives of Black Americans.

▼ These are some of the Black leaders President Franklin D. Roosevelt relied on to advise him on the needs of Black Americans.

## Understanding What You Have Read

A. Write the name of the person next to the statement he or she might have made.

Selma Burke     Mary McLeod Bethune     Eleanor Roosevelt     Richard Wright

_____ 1. I was the head of the Negro Division of the National Youth Administration.

_____ 2. I often talked with Black leaders and supported equal rights for Blacks.

_____ 3. I was a writer who got my start in a New Deal program.

_____ 4. I was paid by the government to make statues.

B. In each of the sentences that follow, the underlined word or words make the sentence true or false. If the sentence is true, write **T** in the blank before it. If it is false, write the word or words that make it true.

_____ 1. The New Deal caused Blacks to support the <u>Republican</u> party.

_____ 2. The relief efforts of the New Deal were particularly aimed at helping <u>Blacks</u>.

_____ 3. The <u>Black Cabinet</u> advised the president on ways the New Deal could help Blacks.

## Using a Chart

Study the chart of these New Deal programs. Then answer the questions.

| Agency or Program | Purpose | Date Founded | Status |
|---|---|---|---|
| Civilian Conservation Corps (CCC) | Provide employment for young men | March 1933 | Ended in 1941 |
| Federal Emergency Relief Administration (FERA) | Provide cash relief to the poor | May 1933 | Ended in 1936 |
| Tennessee Valley Administration (TVA) | Develop the Tennessee Valley | May 1933 | Still operating |
| Public Works Administration (PWA) | Provide employment on public works | June 1933 | Ended in 1937 |
| Federal Deposit Insurance Corporation (FDIC) | Insure bank deposits | June 1933 | Still operating |

1. Which New Deal programs provided employment? _____

_____

2. Which New Deal programs still exist? _____

_____

## Spotlight on People

**Mary McLeod Bethune.** Mary McLeod Bethune was the youngest of 17 children of two former slaves. She spent her early years on her father's small South Carolina farm. By the age of 9, Bethune could pick 250 pounds of cotton a day.

Bethune's parents valued learning as well as hard work and sent Mary to school. She walked five miles a day to the local Black school and she soon advanced to a high level. She won several scholarships to continue her education. One of these was to Chicago's Moody Bible Institute, a training school for missionaries to Africa. Instead of going to Africa as a missionary, Mary started the Daytona (Florida) Normal and Industrial Institute for Negro Girls in 1904.

The school started with only $1.50 in cash, five pupils, and a rented house. She would later remember: "I begged strangers for a broom, a lamp." In 1923, her school became the Bethune-Cookman College. Bethune was its president until 1947. She became known as one of the country's leading Black educators.

Mary McLeod Bethune was an achiever in many areas. She was active in the Black women's movement and served as president of the National Council of Negro Women. During the 1930s, her friendship with Eleanor Roosevelt helped her influence the president. As head of the Negro Affairs division of the National Youth Administration, Bethune helped 600,000 Black children get an education. FDR once told her, "I'm always glad to see you, Mrs. Bethune, for you always come asking for help for others—never for yourself."

One of Mary McLeod Bethune's beliefs was the importance of cooperation among Blacks. Bethune once explained her energy and drive: "The drums of Africa still beat in my heart. They will not let me rest while there is a single Negro boy or girl without a chance to prove his or her worth." Mary McLeod Bethune retired in 1949 but continued to speak out for democratic values until her death in 1955. A national memorial was built in her honor in Washington, D.C., in 1974.

## Recalling the Facts

Choose each correct answer and write the letter in the space provided.

_____ 1. Bethune spent her youth
    a. in a Chicago slum.
    b. on a South Carolina farm.
    c. on an estate in Florida.

_____ 2. Bethune's school began
    a. with little money.
    b. with money from the Moody Bible Institute.
    c. by charging high fees.

_____ 3. Bethune-Cookman College is in
    a. Chicago, Illinois.
    b. Daytona, Florida.
    c. Washington, D.C.

_____ 4. Bethune served as head of the Negro Affairs Division of the
    a. Works Progress Administration.
    b. Civilian Conservation Corps.
    c. National Youth Administration.

_____ 5. Bethune's lifetime goal was to
    a. serve in Africa as a missionary.
    b. sing at the Lincoln Memorial.
    c. obtain training and opportunities for Black youths.

# The Arts and Technology

**Black Artists of the WPA.** The Works Progress Administration (WPA) was the largest, most far-reaching New Deal program. The Federal Art Project was one branch of the WPA. It held art classes for young people with talent. It paid painters to create murals, or large wall paintings, for public places. The Black muralists Charles Wright and Archibald Motley did some of their finest works at the project's mural division in Illinois. Sculptors were paid to carve monuments to famous Americans or scenes from American history. The outpouring of the WPA artists can still be seen in the nation's post offices, court houses, libraries, and airports.

The most famous Black artist of the New Deal period was Jacob Lawrence. He got his start through the Federal Art Project. Lawrence worked in New York. His brightly colored paintings show the sorrows and joys of Black life. One of his most famous paintings is titled *Dancing at the Savoy*. The Savoy was a famous nightclub. Lawrence liked to create paintings around a single theme. He used 60 panels to paint a work titled *Migrations of the Negro*. In two other series, he painted scenes from the lives of Frederick Douglass and Harriet Tubman. In later years, Lawrence illustrated books for children. His work can be seen at the

▲ This is one of the panels of Jacob Lawrence's painting, *The Migration of the Negro*.

Schomberg Center for Research in Black Culture of the New York Public Library. Lawrence's work has been shown at the Seattle Art Museum and the Brooklyn Museum.

Public support for artists during the depression was very important. Because there was little money to spend on basics like food and clothing, the purchase of art became less important. The creation of art remained important, however. Black artists were in an even more difficult position than Whites because they often found it difficult to sell their work. In addition, they had no wealthy patrons to help them. In a difficult time, Black artists created their art with the help of the federal government.

1. Why was government support so important in the development of Black artists and sculptors? _____

_____

2. What was the main theme of Jacob Lawrence's work? _____

## CHAPTER REVIEW: CRITICAL THINKING

1. Many historians believe that the New Deal period was a political turning point for Black Americans. What material discussed in this chapter would support this statement?

_____

_____

2. In your opinion, could the Republican Party have kept the Black vote? If so, how?

_____

_____

# Chapter 10 WORLD WAR II

**AIM: How did World War II affect Black Americans?**

1. World War II was a time when Blacks in the United States made important gains. The war began in Europe in 1939, but the United States did not go to war until 1941. Meanwhile, the United States was building up its defense industries. Thousands of new jobs were created, but Blacks were not being hired for these jobs. Labor leader A. Philip Randolph urged President Roosevelt to change this. When the president did not act, Randolph threatened to lead 100,000 Blacks in a march on Washington. Roosevelt gave in. In June 1941, he ordered defense industries to give fair treatment in hiring to Blacks.

2. The United States entered World War II on December 8, 1941. This was the day after the Japanese had attacked the United States naval

▲ Dorie Miller receives the Navy Cross for extraordinary courage. Three years later he was killed in action.

base at Pearl Harbor, Hawaii. Between then and the end of the war in 1945, one million Blacks served in the armed forces. For most of the war, military units were segregated. Black units were given non-combat duties such as building air strips, driving trucks, and unloading supplies. Even the first Black hero of the war, Dorie Miller, was on non-combat duty when he performed the action that earned him a Navy Cross. Miller was a messman, or kitchen worker, at Pearl Harbor when the Japanese attacked. He seized an anti-aircraft gun from a dying sailor and shot down four Japanese planes. However, he later had to return to duty as a messman.

3. Nevertheless, the armed forces made wider use of Blacks in World War II than they had in World War I. Many Black officers were trained. One of them was Benjamin Oliver Davis. He was an air-combat hero who later became the first Black general in American history. For the first time, Blacks served in the Marine Corps. When Black units were allowed to fight, they were among the best soldiers in the military. Also, more than four thousand Black women joined the newly formed women's branch of the army.

4. On the home front, the war effort created many new jobs. Both Black and White women found a wider variety of jobs than ever before in the defense plants.

5. The changes made during the war also brought some racial tensions. Many southern Whites had moved north to find work. Severe housing shortages, the stresses of wartime, and racial prejudice played a part in causing race riots in some large cities. The worst riot was in Detroit in 1943. More than 40 persons were killed, and hundreds were injured there.

6. In 1944 a Swedish scientist, Gunnar Myrdal, published *An American Dilemma*. His book said that the United States did not practice its ideals. The book awakened many Americans to the issue of racism. As the war ended in 1945, many Americans saw the need to bring about change in their country.

A. Write the name that best completes each sentence in the space provided.

Gunnar Myrdal    A. Philip Randolph    Franklin D. Roosevelt
Dorie Miller    Benjamin Oliver Davis

_____ 1. _____ was the first Black hero of World War II.

_____ 2. _____ ordered American defense industries to hire Blacks.

_____ 3. _____ wrote a book entitled *An American Dilemma*.

_____ 4. _____, air-combat hero of World War II, was the first Black American general.

_____ 5. _____ urged President Roosevelt to change hiring practices in the defense industry.

B. In each of the sentences that follow, the underlined word or words make the sentence true or false. If the sentence is true, write **T** in the blank before it. If it is false, write the word or words that would make it true.

_____ 1. A. Philip Randolph <u>failed</u> in trying to win fair treatment for Blacks in hiring.

_____ 2. Black women <u>were allowed</u> to serve in the women's branch of the army in World War II.

_____ 3. Detroit was <u>the only city</u> where a race riot broke out during the war.

_____ 4. Gunnar Myrdal's book said the United States <u>always</u> put its ideals into practice.

## Linking Past to Present

Study the following time line. Then answer the questions.

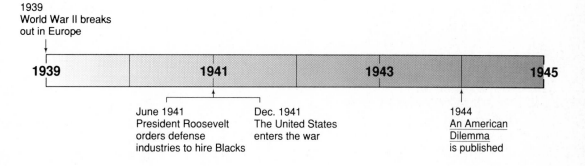

1939
World War II breaks
out in Europe

1939 — 1941 — 1943 — 1945

June 1941
President Roosevelt
orders defense
industries to hire Blacks

Dec. 1941
The United States
enters the war

1944
An American
Dilemma
is published

1. When and where did World War II break out? _____

2. How long before the United States entered the war did the President order defense industries to hire Blacks? _____

3. What book dealt with the issue of race relations? When was it published? _____

4. How many years have passed since the start of World War II? _____

# Spotlight on People

**Charles Richard Drew.** Dr. Charles Drew made one of the most important contributions to the war effort. He worked for years on the problems of blood transfusion. In a **transfusion**, doctors give blood to a person who has lost some in an operation or because of wounds. Dr. Drew found a way to store **plasma**, the part of blood that is clear fluid. Plasma could be set aside and given to the wounded on the battlefield. Dr. Drew's development saved many lives in both war and peace.

Charles Drew grew up in Washington, D.C. He went to Amherst College. There, he played football and took part in track events. After college, Drew was offered a contract to be a football **professional.** He turned it down because he wanted to be a doctor. He received his medical degree from McGill University in Montreal, Canada.

Dr. Drew was one of the first to set up blood banks. These stored blood in case of need. In 1939, he was put in charge of collecting blood for British soldiers. When the United States entered the war, Dr. Drew took over the same job for the American army and navy.

Racists opposed the transfusion of blood from Blacks into Whites. Dr. Drew and others proved that there was no medical difference between "Black" and "White" blood. Even so, blood from Blacks had to be marked for transfusion only to other Blacks. In protest, Dr. Drew quit his job.

Dr. Drew received many awards for his work. He was known as one of the country's best surgeons. He often traveled to speak at meetings of doctors and scientists. In 1950, on a trip to the South, he fell asleep at the wheel of his car and crashed. The hospital where he was taken did not have the plasma that would have saved his life. The man who had saved countless others died because of loss of blood. His contributions live on.

## Recalling the Facts

Choose each correct answer and write the letter in the space provided.

_____ 1. Blood transfusion is
   a. the replacement of blood.
   b. not possible from one person to another.
   c. always dangerous.

_____ 2. Charles Drew turned down an offer to play professional football because
   a. he feared discrimination.
   b. he wanted to become a track star instead.
   c. he wanted to become a doctor.

_____ 3. Dr. Drew found that plasma
   a. could be taken from wounded soldiers.
   b. was not necessary in transfusions.
   c. could be stored.

_____ 4. In World War II, blood from Black soldiers
   a. could not be given to White soldiers.
   b. was not accepted for blood banks.
   c. could be given to anyone.

_____ 5. After World War II, Dr. Drew
   a. refused to work for the government.
   b. stayed in the military.
   c. often lectured to other doctors and scientists.

# Using Primary Sources

**Sarah Tuck.** Sarah Tuck was a 13-year-old girl who lived in a rural town in North Carolina with her father, three younger sisters, and a brother. In 1940, she told Charles S. Johnson, a Black **sociologist,** about her life. A sociologist is a person who studies human society. Here is a section of her story.

> In the summer I do everything—all the washing, cooking and minding the children. I don't mind. Mama taught us all to work before she died.
>
> I just can't stand Mr. Josh—that's the white man where my father works. [He] wanted me to quit school and stay and help his wife wash dishes. He thinks colored don't need to go to school. That's that way he is. Well, I wouldn't do it. . . . I'd cry myself to death if I couldn't go to school. . . .
>
> What I like to do most of all is to go to the movies. About once a month Papa gives me money to go and take all the children. That's the most fun I have. I don't like those western movies, though. The boys go to see them and come home and try to act just like the wild people act in them.
>
> I like school. I failed this year because I had so much to do at home. I felt bad about failing my grade but they are going to give me a chance to take the tests over when the school opens. I try to study my lessons a little every day now, but the children always run in and want something and I never get back to studying. . . . I like school, but I wouldn't want to be no school teacher. I got all the children right here I want to see after. . . .

1. What is Sarah's feeling about school? _____

   _____

2. What keeps Sarah from doing as well as she could in school? _____

   _____

3. What are Sarah's plans for her future? Do you think they are realistic? Explain your

   answer. _____

   _____

## CHAPTER REVIEW: CRITICAL THINKING

1. A. Philip Randolph's threat to lead a protest march on Washington, D.C., came *before* the United States entered World War II. If he had made such a threat *during* the war, how do

   you think Roosevelt would have reacted? _____

   _____

2. A Black woman recalled the war in this way: "No matter what our personal feelings were on the race question, we had to support the nation, because if we lost that, we lost every-

   thing." Explain what she meant. _____

   _____

# Chapter 11 POSTWAR AMERICA

1. One of the goals of Black Americans after World War II was to gain full voting rights in the South. Southerners still did not believe Blacks should vote, even though the Fifteenth Amendment gave them this right. In 1946, Black veterans of World War II marched on the courthouse in Birmingham, Alabama, and tried to register to vote. They were turned away. In some places in the South, Blacks were threatened when they tried to register and vote. Even so, there was some voting by Blacks in the South for the first time since Reconstruction. By 1947, Black voter registration had increased six times over its 1940 level. Still, that meant that only 12 percent of Blacks were registered voters.

2. In the North, Blacks had success in electing Black candidates to public office. In 1945, Adam Clayton Powell, Jr. of New York City and William L. Dawson of Chicago were the two Black members of the United States House of Representatives. Blacks were elected to state legislatures. Blacks also supported White candidates who stood for equal rights.

3. Support for civil rights came from President Harry S Truman. He asked Congress to end the poll tax, pass an anti-lynching law, and set up a permanent Fair Employment Practices Commission. Members of Congress from the South helped prevent these proposals from being made into law. Blacks held protest marches, but the southerners would not bend.

4. Truman used his power as president to act on his own on civil rights. In 1948, he ordered the end of segregation in the armed forces. He also ordered the federal government to hire workers without regard to race. Truman won re-election in 1948. Black voters played a major role in his victory.

5. The economy of the United States boomed in the years after World War II, and many Blacks shared in this prosperity. More Blacks became members of the **middle class**. The middle class includes owners and managers of businesses, clerks and other office workers, teachers, lawyers, physicians, and other professionals. Most Americans are in the middle class. In 1945, John H. Johnson started *Ebony*, a magazine aimed at middle-class Blacks. It became the most successful Black magazine in the United States. Era Bell Thompson, an editor of *Ebony*, wrote about her impressions of Africa. This was part of Black Americans' growing interest in the land of their ancestors.

6. The growth of the Black middle class has been important for Blacks in their fight for equality. Middle-class Blacks have been outspoken in their opposition to segregation. In addition, successful Blacks have served as role models for young people. The Black middle class has also helped to change White views of Blacks. The success of Blacks has helped break down negative attitudes of Whites about the abilities of Blacks. Contacts between the two races have increased. This has helped weaken White fears and reduce prejudice.

▲ Women, Black and White, moved into the work force during and after World War II. These Black women are working in an insurance office

## Understanding What You Have Read

A. In each of the sentences that follow, the underlined word or words make the sentence true or false. If the sentence is true, write **T** in the blank before it. If it is false, write the word or words that would make it true.

_____ 1. Black veterans in the South began to <u>demand</u> their right to vote.

_____ 2. Southern members of Congress <u>helped to pass</u> civil rights laws for Blacks.

_____ 3. President Truman <u>opposed</u> the cause of Black rights.

_____ 4. There were <u>fewer</u> Blacks in the middle class in the post-war years.

_____ 5. As more Blacks became successful, Whites began to <u>change</u> their attitudes toward Blacks.

B. Write the name that best completes each sentence in the space provided.

Adam Clayton Powell, Jr.    Era Bell Thompson    Fair Employment Practices
Birmingham, Alabama    John H. Johnson       Commission

_____ 1. President Truman tried to set up the _____ as part of a civil rights program.

_____ 2. A member of Congress from New York City in 1945 was _____ .

_____ 3. _____ was a magazine editor who wrote about Africa.

_____ 4. Black war veterans marched on the courthouse in _____ to try to register to vote.

_____ 5. The man who founded *Ebony* magazine was _____ .

## Daily Life

**The Apollo Theater.** In 1934, a new theater opened in New York City's Harlem. It was called the Apollo. The best Black entertainment of the day appeared at the Apollo. Its popularity continued through World War II and continues to this day. Harlemites came to enjoy the music and see friends.

Amateur Night at the Apollo was a ticket to fame for many young people. In 1942, an 18-year-old named Sarah Vaughan took up a friend's dare and entered the Amateur Night contest. She sang "Body and Soul" and won the contest. The 1950s and 1960s saw the Apollo introduce young singers like Gladys Knight, James Brown, and Dionne Warwick. The comedian and actor Richard Pryor was an Apollo "find."

1. The Apollo Theater is in _____ .

2. The singer _____ made her debut in 1942 at an Apollo contest.

3. Other performers introduced at the Apollo Theater are

_____ .

▲ Harlemites enjoyed the best Black entertainers at the Apollo Theater.

## Spotlight on People

**Jackie Robinson.** Professional baseball had been segregated from the time it began. All-Black teams first began in 1885. Black teams played against each other in Black leagues. Black stars were widely thought to be as good as the best White "major leaguers." Josh Gibson was known as the Black Babe Ruth. But no White team dared to risk public disapproval by hiring Black players.

In 1945, Branch Rickey, the general manager of the White Brooklyn Dodgers, signed Jackie Robinson to a minor-league contract. Robinson had been a great all-round athlete at the University of California at Los Angeles. He first played for the Kansas City Monarchs of the Negro American League.

Rickey sent Robinson to play with the Dodgers' minor-league team in Montreal, Canada. In the 1940s, racial prejudice was not as great in Canada as in the United States.

The test came in 1947, when Robinson joined the Dodgers as a second baseman. Robinson had to take insults from fans, opposing players, and even some of his own teammates. In some cities, he had to stay in a separate hotel from his White teammates.

Robinson's courage and skills as a player won him respect. In 1949 he was named the Most Valuable Player in the National League. Soon, other teams began to sign Black players. Together, Jackie Robinson and Branch Rickey had broken the "color line" for good.

Robinson led the Dodgers to six pennants and one World Series title. He retired in 1956 and became vice-president of a New York restaurant chain. In 1962, Jackie Robinson became the first Black named to the Baseball Hall of Fame. He died in 1972. By then, Black stars such as Willie Mays and Hank Aaron were earning salaries as high as those of any White players. Black players were on every team. In 1974, Frank Robinson became the first Black manager of a major-league team, the Cleveland Indians.

## Recalling the Facts

Choose each correct answer and write the letter in the space provided.

_____ 1. Blacks played on separate baseball teams
   a. from the time pro baseball began.
   b. because they were not good as Whites.
   c. because they did not earn enough money.

_____ 2. Robinson was sent to the minor-league team in Montreal because
   a. he had to learn to play baseball.
   b. no one there knew who he was.
   c. there was less prejudice in Canada in the 1940s.

_____ 3. When Robinson came to the White major leagues,
   a. the fans welcomed him.
   b. his teammates protected him.
   c. he faced prejudice from both fans and teammates.

_____ 4. After Robinson entered the major leagues,
   a. no other Blacks were allowed to play.
   b. many more Blacks entered the major leagues.
   c. only a few Blacks were allowed to play.

# The Arts and Technology

**Black Novels.** In the 1940s and 1950s, two talented Black writers of novels drew the praise of America's readers. One of them was Richard Wright. His books *Native Son* and *Black Boy* told what it was like being Black in a White world. The other writer was Ralph Ellison. In 1952, Ellison's novel *Invisible Man* was published. It was his first novel and drew great praise. The following is a sample of the opening lines of *Invisible Man*:

> I am an invisible man. No, I am not a spook like those who haunted Edgar Allan Poe; nor am I one of your Hollywood movie ectoplasms. I am a man of substance, of flesh and bone, fiber and liquids—and I might even be said to possess a mind. I am invisible, understand, simply because people refuse to see me. . . . When they approach me they see only my surroundings, themselves, or figments of their imagination—indeed, everything and anything except me. . . .
>
> I am not complaining, nor am I protesting either. It is sometimes advantageous to be unseen, although it is most often rather wearing on the nerves. Then too, you're constantly being bumped against by those of poor vision. Or again, you often doubt if you really exist.

Ralph Ellison is the author of *Invisible Man*, an American masterpiece. ▶

### Vocabulary

**ectoplasm** a ghost    **advantageous** helpful    **anguish** suffering
**figment** an invention    **phantom** a ghost

Is the character in Ellison's novel really invisible? Why does he say he is? _____

_____

## CHAPTER REVIEW: CRITICAL THINKING

1.  Assume you are a Black who has just returned home from army service in World War II. What progress would you expect to be made in the situation of Blacks in the postwar years?

    To what extent are your expectations realized? _____

    _____

    _____

2.  Of the people mentioned in this chapter, which one do you admire most? Explain why.

    _____

    _____

# UNIT 3 REVIEW

## Summary of the Unit

A few of the most important events and facts presented in Unit 3 are listed below. Write the events and facts in your notebook and add three more.

1. Blacks suffered from the economic hardships of the Great Depression.
2. The New Deal programs of Franklin D. Roosevelt included many benefits for Blacks.
3. Blacks served in all branches of the armed forces during World War II. Many Blacks at home found jobs in defense industries.
4. After World War II, more Blacks began to move into the middle class.

## Understanding What You Have Read

Write the letter of the answer that best completes each sentence in the space provided.

_____ 1. One of he first labor unions for Blacks was the
    a. Brotherhood of Sleeping Car Porters.
    b. American Federation of Labor.
    c. Congress of Industrial Organizations.

_____ 2. The Black Cabinet was
    a. a religious group.
    b. an informal group of advisors to President Franklin D. Roosevelt.
    c. a federal relief agency.

_____ 3. A majority of Blacks began to vote for the Democratic party
    a. during President Truman's administration.
    b. during the 1920s.
    c. during President Franklin D. Roosevelt's administration.

_____ 4. During most of World War II, Blacks served
    a. mostly in segregated units.
    b. in integrated units.
    c. only in the army.

_____ 5. President Truman
    a. faced opposition on civil rights from northern congressmen.
    b. set up a Fair Employment Practices Commission.
    c. supported civil rights.

_____ 6. After World War II,
    a. more Blacks became middle class.
    b. Blacks were poorer than ever.
    c. there were very few poor Blacks.

## Building Your Vocabulary

Complete each of the following sentences by writing one of these words or terms in the space provided.

        middle class    labor union    New Deal
        messman       depression      blues

1. A _____ is a kitchen worker on a ship.

2. People who work as professionals belong to the _____.

3. A time when many people are out of work and there is a great deal of economic hardship is called a _____.

4. President Franklin D. Roosevelt's program to lift the United States out of the Great Depression is called the _____.

5. The kind of music that expresses personal sorrow and loneliness is called the _____.

6. The organization that helps workers fight for higher wages and greater security is called

   a _____.

## Developing Ideas and Skills—Making a Time Line

Study the following list of events and dates. In the space below, make a time line with the events in the order they occurred.

1. A majority of Blacks first voted for the Democratic candidate in the presidential election of 1936.
2. Japan attacked the American base of Pearl Harbor in 1941. The United States entered World War II.
3. Franklin D. Roosevelt was first elected president in 1932.
4. The stock market crashed in 1929. The depression began soon afterward.
5. In 1933, President Roosevelt's New Deal programs began.

## Making History Live

1. Choose one of the incidents described in this unit and prepare a dramatization of it to perform before your class.
2. Report on the life and work of one of the following: Marian Anderson, Jacob Lawrence, Sarah Vaughan, A. Philip Randolph, General Benjamin O. Davis, Father Divine (George Baker), Jackie Robinson, Richard Wright, Ralph Ellison.

# THE SUPREME COURT ACTS

Chapter **12**

**AIM: What part did the Supreme Court play in granting civil rights to Blacks?**

1. In 1935, the National Association for the Advancement of Colored People (NAACP) began to challenge the "separate but equal" rule in the courts. This rule said that the Jim Crow laws were legal. Two NAACP lawyers led this fight. They were Charles Hamilton Houston and Thurgood Marshall. They sued states that did not have equal facilities for Blacks. In education, they concentrated on state colleges. By 1950 some southern colleges had let in Black students. But public schools in many states were still segregated.

2. In the 1950s, the NAACP sued the Board of Education of Topeka, Kansas. One Black student, Linda Brown, had not been permitted to attend an all-white public school. In 1954, the case, *Brown v. Board of Education*, reached the Supreme Court. Thurgood Marshall argued that segregation itself kept Blacks from getting an equal education. The court agreed. it unanimously, or without disagreement, struck down the "separate but equal" rule.

▲ Little did nine-year-old Linda Brown realize that her name would go down in history when she tried to enroll in an elementary school in Topeka, Kansas.

Chief Justice Earl Warren, who wrote the court's decision, said, "Education is perhaps the most important function of the state.... The opportunity of an education ... is a right which must be made available to all on equal terms." The court said that separate educational facilities are by their very nature unequal. Therefore, *all* school segregation laws violated the Constitution.

3. A year later the Supreme Court told the states to obey the Brown decision and desegregate the schools "with all deliberate speed." Eventually the ruling was extended to all public facilities. It was the end of one era, the beginning of another. The civil rights gains that followed are sometimes called "the second Reconstruction."

4. Reaction to the Brown decision varied. Black Americans and Whites who believed in equality were delighted. Border states such as Maryland made plans to desegregate, or **integrate**, their schools. However, in the Deep South, opposition to the decision was strong. Many communities in the North also opposed the decision.

5. In 1957, President Dwight D. Eisenhower put the power of the federal government behind the Supreme Court's decision. Nine black students tried to enroll in the all-White high school in Little Rock, Arkansas. White parents blocked the entrance. The Arkansas governor, Orval Faubus, called out the Arkansas National Guard to keep the Black students from entering the school. President Eisenhower then sent federal troops to Little Rock to make sure that the court's order would be obeyed. The Black students entered while the troops stood on guard. This was the first use of federal troops to defend Black civil rights since Reconstruction.

6. The Brown Supreme Court decision made school segregation illegal. However, actual integration of the schools took many years to accomplish in both the North and the South. By 1970 almost all schools in the United States were open to Blacks and Whites.

## Understanding What You Have Read

A. Place the name of the person below next to the statement that describes each person.

Earl Warren      Thurgood Marshall    Linda Brown
Dwight Eisenhower   Orval Faubus

_____ 1. I sent federal troops to Little Rock to enforce the Supreme Court order to desegregate schools.

_____ 2. I was the student who was kept out of White schools in Topeka, Kansas.

_____ 3. I argued the case for the NAACP in *Brown v. Board of Education.*

_____ 4. I wrote the Supreme Court decision in *Brown v. Board of Education.*

_____ 5. I was the Arkansas governor who sent the National Guard to keep Black students out of Little Rock High School.

B. In each of the sentences that follow, the underlined word or words make the sentence true or false. If the sentence is true, write **T** in the blank before it. If it is false, write the word or words that make it true.

_____ 1. Thurgood Marshall argued that segregation <u>allowed</u> equal education for Blacks.

_____ 2. In the case of *Brown v. Board of Education,* the Supreme Court <u>approved</u> the "seperate but equal" rule.

_____ 3. The schools in both the North and the South did not desegregate <u>immediately</u> after the Brown decision.

## Building Geography Skills

Study the map on this page. Then answer the questions.

1. Name five states where public schools were segregated by law before 1954. _____

_____

2. Were the public schools in your state segregated or open to all races before 1954? _____

_____

3. Name the two states closest to you where public schools were open to all before 1954. _____

4. Which states allowed local officials to set school policy on segregation? _____

**School Segregation Before 1954**

CANADA

0    400 Miles
0    400 Kilometers

☐ Public schools open to all.  ■ Separate schools for blacks required by state law  ☐ Segregation optional at the local level

## Spotlight on People

**Thurgood Marshall.** Thurgood Marshall's grandfather was born in Africa and brought to America as a slave. Marshall's mother was a teacher, and his father was a country-club steward. Thurgood Marshall became the first Black to sit on the nation's highest court.

Marshall got his law degree at Howard University, an all-Black college in Washington, D.C. The head of the law school was Charles Hamilton Houston. When Houston became the chief lawyer for the NAACP, he hired Marshall as his assistant. They sued states that did not have law schools for Blacks. The courts had to agree that these states did not have "separate but equal" facilities. In one case, the state of Missouri offered to build a law school just for one Black student to prevent him from going to the all-White law school. In another case, courts ordered the University of Oklahoma to admit a Black student.

But the school made him use a desk marked "Reserved for Colored."

Marshall and other NAACP lawyers had long wanted to try to overturn the "separate but equal" rule completely. Marshall decided to try to prove that segregated public schools were unconstitutional. The opportunity came when Linda Brown was not allowed to attend an all-White school in Topeka, Kansas. The case reached the Supreme Court.

Marshall showed that states with segregated schools spent far less for Black students than for White students. He called experts who told the court that being in a segregated school damaged the self-image of Blacks. The Black students knew that they were being set apart as inferiors. The Supreme Court agreed and ruled that segregated schools must be abolished.

President John F. Kennedy appointed Marshall a federal judge in 1961. He left his post in 1965 to become solicitor general, or chief trial lawyer, of the Justice Department. Two years later, president Lyndon B. Johnson named Marshall to the Supreme Court. Over the years, Thurgood Marshall has been a powerful voice on the court for minority rights.

## Recalling the Facts

Choose each correct answer and write the letter in the space provided.

_____ 1. The states that Charles Hamilton Houston and Marshall sued
   a. had no grade schools for Blacks.
   b. kept Blacks out of all schools.
   c. had no law schools for Blacks.

_____ 2. Marshall showed that states with segregated schools
   a. spent less for White students than for Blacks.
   b. spent about the same for both Whites and Blacks.
   c. spent less for Black students than for Whites.

_____ 3. Marshall's grandfather was a
   a. slave.
   b. country-club steward.
   c. law school teacher.

_____ 4. Experts testified that segregated schools hurt Blacks' self-image because
   a. they knew they were thought to be inferior.
   b. they were angry at being separated from Whites.
   c. they had no way of knowing what Whites were like.

# The Arts and Technology

**Playwriting.** In 1959, a play called *A Raisin in the Sun* opened on Broadway and quickly became a hit. The play was written by a Black woman and it told about an ordinary Black family. Plays by Black women and about Black families were hardly ever seen on Broadway or ever became successful.

The author of the play was Lorraine Hansberry. She was talented in many fields. Born in Chicago in 1930, she studied at the University of Wisconsin and the Art Institute of Chicago. She went to New York City to try to start a career as a writer. She worked at many jobs before she became successful. She was a department store clerk, waitress, cashier, and hostess in a restaurant.

Hansberry took the title of her play from a poem by Langston Hughes: "What happens to a dream deferred [put off for later]? / Does it dry up / like a raisin in the sun?" The play's opening saw the first Broadway appearance of the young actor Sidney Poitier. The play tells of a Chicago family that has received a large sum of money. The main characters are a mother, her son, and her daughter. They have different ideas on

▲ This is a tense scene from *A Raisin in the Sun.*

how the money should be used. The audience comes to understand the difference between the older and younger generations. The play also shows the family's ideas about the American dream of success.

A critic once told Hansberry that her play was not "really a Negro play. Why, this could be about anybody! It's a play about people." Hansberry replied, "Well, I hadn't noticed the contradiction, because I'd always been under the impression that Negroes are people."

1. How do you know that Lorraine Hansberry was not easily discouraged? _____

_____

2. What did the critic mean when he said Hansberry's play "could be about anybody"?

_____

3. What is the main conflict of *A Raisin in the Sun*? _____

_____

## CHAPTER REVIEW: CRITICAL THINKING

The Black writer Louis Lomax wrote this about the Supreme Court's decision in *Brown v. Board of Education:* "That was the day we won; the day we took the White man's laws and won our case before an all-White Supreme Court with a proud Negro lawyer. . . . And were proud."

1. How did the reaction of Blacks such as Lomax help the cause of Black rights? _____

_____

2. Did only Blacks have a reason to be proud of the Brown decision? Why? _____

_____

# Chapter 13 A TIME FOR PROTEST

**AIM: How did Blacks in the South use direct action to gain their rights?**

1. A new stage in the civil rights struggle began on December 1, 1955. In Montgomery, Alabama, a Black woman named Rosa Parks took a seat on a city bus. The bus became crowded. The driver told her to give up her seat to a White man and move to the back. By law all Blacks were supposed to move to the back of the bus so that Whites could sit up front. Parks refused. The bus driver had her arrested for breaking the city's segregation law. Montgomery's Black leaders decided to protest. They called on Blacks to boycott, or not use, the bus system until they were treated fairly. Blacks walked or used car pools. A young minister became leader of the boycott. His name was Dr. Martin Luther King, Jr. City officials tried to break the movement by sending its leaders to jail. In November 1956, the Supreme Court ruled that segregation in transportation was illegal. The city ended its Jim Crow travel laws. The bus company gave in and desegregated its system.

2. In 1957, several Black church groups formed the Southern Christian Leadership Conference (SCLC). Dr. King was its head. The SCLC's aim was to desegregate facilities in other southern cities through peaceful means. The SCLC started boycotts, demonstrations, and voter registration drives.

3. On February 1, 1960, four Black college students sat at the lunch counter of a store in Greensboro, North Carolina. They ordered coffee. As they expected, the store would not serve them because they were Black. However, they stayed in their seats until the store closed. In a few days **"sit-ins"** like the one in Greensboro spread across the South. In April 1960, some of the students formed the Student Non-violent Coordinating Committee (SNCC). By 1962, SNCC had used the sit-in tactic to integrate other public facilities in more than 100 cities.

4. Another protest tactic was the Freedom Ride. This was used by the Congress of Racial Equality (CORE), headed by James Farmer. In 1961, thousands of Blacks and Whites rode buses and trains in the South. These Freedom Riders wanted to show that court rulings against segregation in transportation were not being obeyed. The Freedom Riders met violent resistance. President John F. Kennedy sent federal marshals to protect them. The Freedom Ride movement spread.

5. In May 1963, civil rights marchers began to parade through Birmingham, Alabama. The police used high-pressure hoses, dogs, and cattle prods against them. Pictures of this violence won support for the civil rights movement throughout the country.

6. In 1963, A. Philip Randolph, the union leader, and other civil rights leaders called for a march on Washington, D.C. The purpose of the march was to influence Congress to pass new laws against segregation. On August 28, 1963, around 250,000 people gathered in front of the Lincoln Memorial in the nation's capital as millions of Americans watched on television. The high point of the march was Dr. King's famous speech, "I Have a Dream." This event is remembered as the peak of the civil rights movement of our time.

▲ Rosa Parks being interviewed after she was arrested for breaking a Jim Crow law in Montgomery, Alabama

## Understanding What You Have Read

A. Write the name of the person next to the statement he or she might have made.

Rosa Parks     Dr. Martin Luther King, Jr.     John F. Kennedy
James Farmer     A. Philip Randolph

_____ 1. I sent federal marshals to Montgomery to protect Freedom Riders.

_____ 2. I was the leader of the Congress of Racial Equality.

_____ 3. I refused to give my seat on a bus to a White man.

_____ 4. I called people to march on Washington in 1963.

_____ 5. I was the first head of the Southern Christian Leadership Conference.

B. In each of the sentences that follow, the underlined word makes the statement true or false. If the sentence is true, write T in the blank before it. If it is false, write the word that makes it true.

_____ 1. The Montgomery bus boycott ended when the bus company gave in.

_____ 2. The Freedom Riders were welcomed in the South.

_____ 3. The purpose of the 1963 March on Washington was to influence Congress to pass laws against segregation.

_____ 4. The sit-in students wanted to segregate public facilities.

## Linking Past to Present

Study the time line. Then complete each sentence.

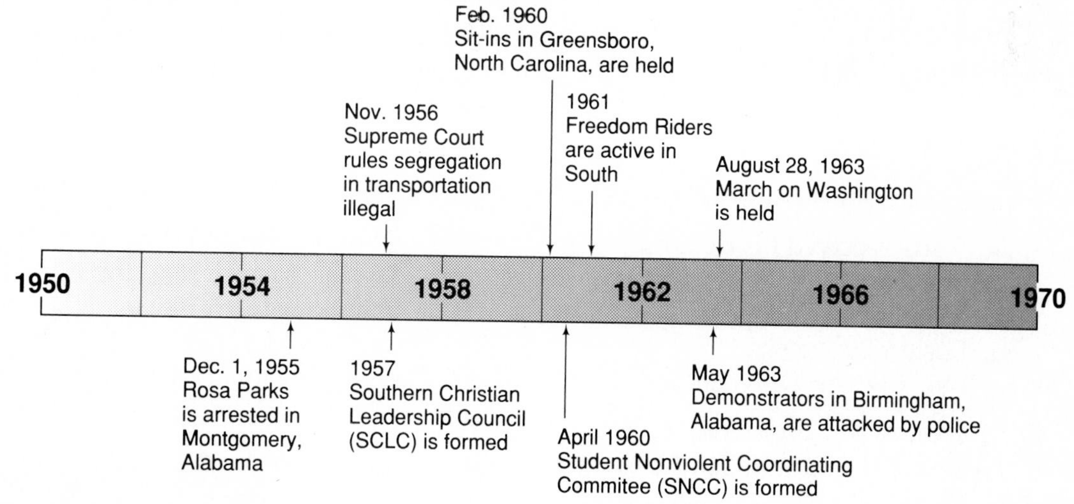

Feb. 1960
Sit-ins in Greensboro,
North Carolina, are held

Nov. 1956
Supreme Court
rules segregation
in transportation
illegal

1961
Freedom Riders
are active in
South

August 28, 1963
March on Washington
is held

| 1950 | 1954 | 1958 | 1962 | 1966 | 1970 |
|------|------|------|------|------|------|

Dec. 1, 1955
Rosa Parks
is arrested in
Montgomery,
Alabama

1957
Southern Christian
Leadership Council
(SCLC) is formed

April 1960
Student Nonviolent Coordinating
Commitee (SNCC) is formed

May 1963
Demonstrators in Birmingham,
Alabama, are attacked by police

1. When were the police active against civil rights? _____

2. How long after the formation of the SCLC was the march on Washington held?

_____

3. How long after the Supreme Court decision did the Freedom Riders demonstrate?

_____

4. How long ago was Rosa Parks arrested? _____

# Spotlight on People

**Martin Luther King, Jr.** Martin Luther King, Jr., was born in Atlanta, Georgia, in 1929. He entered Morehouse College in Atlanta at age 15. After becoming a minister, he continued his studies at Crozer Theological Seminary in Pennsylvania. There, he learned of the teachings of Mohandas K. Gandhi.

Gandhi was a Hindu leader who had shown the power of nonviolence in winning independence for India in 1947. King saw that the Black struggle in the United States was a moral one. He decided it could not succeed by using immoral methods. He decided never to use violence.

While studying for his doctoral degree at Boston University, King met Coretta Scott. A talented singer, she was training for a concert career. She gave it up to become King's wife in 1953. The next year King was named minister of the Dexter Avenue Baptist Church in Montgomery, Alabama.

Dr. King's decision never to use violence was not an easy idea to follow. In the civil rights demonstrations, he faced dogs, clubs, and insults of Whites. The temptation to fight back was strong. Yet King declared, "We will not resort to violence. We will not degrade ourselves with hatred. Love will be returned for hate." In 1964, Dr. King received the Nobel Peace Prize.

On April 4, 1968, Dr. King was killed in Memphis, Tennessee, by a White escaped convict.

Today, the birthday in January of this great civil rights leader is a national holiday.

## Recalling the Facts

Choose each correct answer and write the letter in the space provided.

_____ 1. Dr. King received his doctoral degree from
　　**a.** Morehouse College.
　　**b.** Boston University.
　　**c.** Buckingham University.

_____ 2. Mohandas K. Gandhi led
　　**a.** a non-violent independence movement.
　　**b.** the boycott in Montgomery, Alabama.
　　**c.** a group that practiced violence.

_____ 3. Dr. King told others to return hate with
　　**a.** love.
　　**b.** more hate.
　　**c.** attacks.

_____ 4. Dr. King resisted those
　　**a.** who tried to send him to jail.
　　**b.** who wanted to use peaceful methods.
　　**c.** who wanted to use violent methods.

_____ 5. Just before his death, Dr. King thought
　　**a.** he had been a failure.
　　**b.** he should change his ideas.
　　**c.** victory was in sight.

# Using Primary Sources

The speech that Dr. Martin Luther King, Jr., made at the Lincoln Memorial in 1963 was a high point of his career. Here is a part of it.

I have a dream that one day on the red hills of Georgia sons of former slaves and the sons of former slaveowners will be able to sit down together at the table of brotherhood. . . .

I have a dream that one day this nation will rise up and live out the true meaning of its creed. We hold these truths to be self-evident that all men are created equal. . . .

I have a dream that my little children will one day live in a nation where they will not be judged by the color of their skin but by the content of their character. . . .

This is our hope. This is the faith that I will go back to the South with. With this faith we will be able to hew out of the mountain of despair a stone of hope. . . ."

▲ Some of the thousands of Americans who came to the nation's capital to take part in the March on Washington.

1. What was King's dream for the southern Whites who opposed civil rights for Blacks?

_____

_____

2. What was King's dream for his own children? _____

_____

## CHAPTER REVIEW: CRITICAL THINKING

Dr. King once said, "Three simple words describe . . . what Negroes really want. The words are *all*, *now*, and *here*"

1. Explain what he meant by this statement. _____

_____

2. What factors made the civil rights movement successful after World War II? _____

_____

# 14 THE CIVIL RIGHTS MOVEMENT HEATS UP

AIM: What changes took place in the civil rights movement after 1963? Why did these changes take place?

1. On November 22, 1963, President John F. Kennedy was killed. The nation was shocked. Many Blacks had seen him as a friend. The new president, Lyndon B. Johnson, was from the South. Nevertheless, he strongly backed Kennedy's civil rights bill. Congress passed it in August 1964. The new Civil Rights Act was the most important civil rights law since Reconstruction. It outlawed discrimination in public places. These included public swimming pools, theaters, and restaurants. The law forbade employers and unions from discriminating against Blacks. No one would be denied a job or kept from attending a school because of race or religion.

2. Even so, White southerners denied Blacks voting rights in many places. Without the right to vote, Blacks would not be elected to public office. In 1964, volunteers from all over the country went to the South for what was called the Freedom Summer project. They tried to register Black voters. White officials refused to obey the Civil Rights Act. A terror campaign began against the registration drive. Thirty-five churches were burned. Several people were murdered. The violence continued the next year in Selma, Alabama. Marchers walking from Selma to the state capital in Montgomery were attacked by state troopers using clubs and tear gas. TV reports of the attack saddened the country.

3. In response, Congress passed the Voting Rights Act of 1965. It gave the federal government power to enforce voter registration. All tests for voting were outlawed. The law was effective. By 1968, more than half the Blacks of voting age were registered.

4. Blacks, especially young people, were impatient with the slow progress of the civil rights movement. Many became **militant**. A militant person is one who is ready to fight for a cause. Radicals in SNCC and CORE took up the slogan "Black Power." Leaders like Stokely Carmichael said Blacks should control their own communities and organizations. SNCC and CORE threw out their White members. Black militants called for greater Black economic power. Some militant leaders turned away from Dr. King's nonviolent ideas. The Black Panther Party, which started in 1966, believed that Blacks should strike back or defend themselves against attacks by Whites.

5. The Black Power movement created the idea that "Black is Beautiful." Instead of imitating Whites, Blacks now stressed their own cultural, musical, and artistic heritage. Some wore their hair in "Afros" and wore African-style dashikis, or loose-fitting garments. Some Blacks adopted African names. They began to demand that Black Studies, or courses in Black culture and history, be taught in schools and colleges.

6. In northern urban areas, conditions for Blacks did not improve. Riots broke out when Blacks became angry with police brutality, bad schools, poor housing, and continued low economic standards. The first major riot broke out in 1965 in the Watts section of Los Angeles. The largest riots were in Detroit, Michigan, and Newark, New Jersey, in 1967. Stores and houses were burned. Many people were killed. Such violence frightened many Whites. Black Power seemed a threatening slogan to them.

▲ Dr. Martin Luther King, Jr., and Coretta Scott King lead the marchers in Selma before the attack by the police.

## Understanding What You Have Read

A. Next to each item in Column A, write the letter of the item in Column B that explains it.

<table>
<tr><td colspan="2">Column A</td><td>Column B</td></tr>
<tr><td>_____ 1.</td><td>Voting Rights Act of 1965</td><td>a. outlawed discrimination in public places</td></tr>
<tr><td>_____ 2.</td><td>Black Power</td><td>b. scene of 1965 riot</td></tr>
<tr><td>_____ 3.</td><td>Watts</td><td>c. policy of radicals in SNCC and CORE</td></tr>
<tr><td>_____ 4.</td><td>Civil Rights Act of 1964</td><td>d. allowed the federal government to examine voter registration practices</td></tr>
<tr><td>_____ 5.</td><td>"Black is Beautiful."</td><td>e. slogan of those who thought Blacks should value themselves and their history</td></tr>
<tr><td>_____ 6.</td><td>Freedom Summer project</td><td>f. volunteer program to register Black voters</td></tr>
</table>

B. In each of the sentences that follow, the underlined word or words make the sentence true or false. If the sentence is true, write **T** in the blank before it. If it is false, write the word or words that make it true.

_____ 1. The Civil Rights Act of 1964 <u>allowed</u> employers and unions to discriminate.

_____ 2. Some Black radicals thought Blacks <u>should</u> take power without Whites' help.

_____ 3. In 1967, <u>Detroit and Newark</u> were the scene of large-scale riots.

_____ 4. Generally, militant leaders <u>supported</u> Dr. King's nonviolent ideas.

# Building Geography Skills

Study the map on this page. Then answer the questions.

1. Name two cities on the Great Lakes where people died in the civil rights riots of the 1960s. _____

_____

2. In what western cities did riots occur?

_____

_____

3. How many riots does the map show for the South? _____

4. Which part of the United States saw the most civil rights riots in the 1960s?

_____

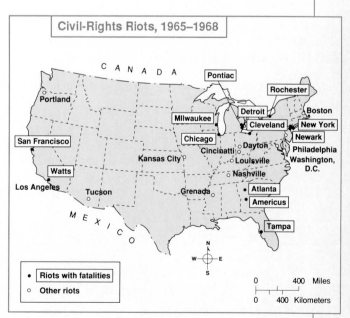

Civil-Rights Riots, 1965–1968

61 ▶

# Spotlight on People

**Fannie Lou Hamer.** Fannie Lou Hamer's life shows the changes the civil rights movement brought about. Born in Sunflower County, Mississippi, in 1917, she was the youngest of 20 children. Her parents were poor farmers. Hamer had little education. She worked in the cotton fields as a time keeper.

In 1962, Hamer heard of the SNCC voter-registration drive. She and 17 other Blacks went to Ruleville, the county seat, to register. When she returned to her job, her boss said, "We are not ready for this in Mississippi" and gave her the choice of voting or keeping her job. She left and stayed at a friend's house. Later, someone fired a gun at the house. Hamer had to leave the county for her own safety.

However, she returned to Ruleville and registered. Some friends thought she was brave. Others thought she was foolish. She said she was "just sick and tired of being sick and tired." She became a worker for SNCC.

The summer of 1963 was difficult for Black civil rights workers. Medgar Evers, the head of the state NAACP, was shot and killed. Because she worked for SNCC, Hamer was arrested and severely beaten with leather straps.

In 1964, Hamer helped set up the Mississippi Freedom Democratic Party (MFDC). The MFDC sent its own delegates to the Democratic national convention that year. They challenged the White delegates from Mississippi. They wanted the places that were set aside for Mississippi. The "regulars" were barred because the Mississippi Democratic Party had long discriminated against Blacks.

The civil rights movement forced Mississippi to change its ways. In 1970, Ruleville held a Fannie Lou Hamer Day. Both Whites and Blacks attended. The White mayor, who would not speak to Hamer just two years before, now described her as a champion of her people. Hamer said, "If you just stand there and don't lash back, you can find a real human being in a lot of people. I don't never write nobody off." Seven years later Hamer died of cancer. The Mississippi legislature praised her service to the state.

## Recalling the Facts

Choose each correct answer and write the letter in the space provided.

_____ 1. Hamer's boss gave her the choice of
   a. voting or keeping her job.
   b. staying at home or working for him.
   c. getting a good job or leaving home.

_____ 2. Because Hamer worked for SNCC,
   a. she became mayor of Ruleville.
   b. she was driven out of Mississippi.
   c. she was arrested and beaten.

_____ 3. The Mississippi Freedom Democratic Party
   a. challenged the convention delegates from the regular Democratic Party.
   b. was never allowed into a Democratic Party convention.
   c. discriminated against Blacks.

_____ 4. In 1970, Ruleville's attitudes toward Blacks
   a. were still the same as ever.
   b. were worse than before the civil rights movement.
   c. had changed for the better.

## Using Primary Sources

The violent attack on the marchers at Selma, Alabama in March 1965 shocked Americans. On that "Bloody Sunday," eight-year-old Sheyann Webb was one of the marchers. Years later, she recalled what happened.

All I knew is I heard all this screaming and the people were turning and I saw this first part of the line running and stumbling back toward us. . . . And they came running and some of them were crying out and somebody yelled, "Oh, God, they're killing us!" I think I just froze then. There were people everywhere, jamming against me, pushing against me. . . . It seemed like just a few seconds went by and I heard a shout. "Gas! Gas!" And everybody started screaming again. And I looked and I saw the [Alabama state] troopers charging us again and some of them were . . . throwing canisters [cans]of tear gas. And beyond them I saw the horsemen starting their charge toward us. I was terrified. What happened then is something I'll never forget as long as I live. Never. In fact, I still dream about it sometimes.

I saw those horsemen coming toward me and they had those awful masks on; they rode right through the cloud of tear gas.

. . . I just turned and ran. And just as I was turning the tear gas got me; it burned my nose first and then got my eyes. I was blinded by the tears. . . . I don't know if I was screaming or not, but everyone else was. People were running and falling and ducking. . . . It was like a nightmare seeing it through the tears. . . .

1. What caused the people at the front of the line to turn back? _____

   _____

2. Why were the horsemen able to ride into the cloud of tear gas? _____

   _____

## CHAPTER REVIEW: CRITICAL THINKING

The Black Power movement was part of a long argument that began in the nineteenth century and continued with Marcus Garvey.

1. Should the goal of Blacks be integration or Black nationalism? Which approach do you

   favor? Explain why. _____

   _____

2. Explain how the idea "Black is Beautiful" relates to the ideas of earlier Black leaders.

   _____

   _____

# THE VIETNAM WAR

**AIM: What part did Blacks play in the Vietnam War? How did the Vietnam War affect the civil rights movement?**

1. Vietnam is a country in Southeast Asia. In 1954 it had been divided into two parts. North Vietnam was led by communists. South Vietnam was non-communist, but rebels there sided with North Vietnam communists. To keep South Vietnam from turning communist, the United States decided to back the government there. In 1965, President Lyndon Johnson sent the first combat troops to South Vietnam. By the time America's part in the war ended in 1973, over three million American troops had served in Vietnam.

2. The war in Vietnam was the first war in which all military units were integrated. More Blacks were officers than in previous wars. Many Black soldiers won medals for bravery. Blacks made up a greater percentage of the combat forces than in any earlier war, but they

▲ American soldiers on patrol in Vietnam. The Vietnam War was the first war in which the armed forces were completely integrated.

paid a high price. Blacks had a higher rate of casualties, wounded and killed, than Whites.

3. As the war grew, many Americans began to think that our involvement was wrong. An anti-war movement began. Blacks faced a problem. President Johnson had staked his prestige on the war. Black leaders knew that Johnson had backed the cause of civil rights. They did not want to appear unpatriotic. But some Blacks felt that the real enemy was racism and poverty at home. Some saw the war as a racist one, against an Asiatic people.

4. In 1967, Dr. Martin Luther King, Jr., broke with President Johnson on the war. King felt the costs of the war, in money and men, were too high. The war took away from the fight against poverty and injustice at home. Dr. King's views had a strong influence on Black attitudes.

5. The year 1968 was a year of turmoil. Anti-war protests came to a head in 1968. Dr. King was assassinated on April 4. The killing set off riots all across the country. In June of that year, Robert F. Kennedy, the brother of President John F. Kennedy, was assassinated while running for the Democratic nomination for president. Later in the year, the Democratic convention in Chicago was rocked by violence and protests. The result was the election of Richard Nixon as president.

6. Nixon slowly took steps to remove American troops from the war. With no hope for victory, morale in the armed forces dropped. Conflicts between Black and White soldiers increased. Worse yet, some soldiers, both Black and White, developed a drug habit.

7. When the Vietnam veterans returned home, they suffered from many problems. Black veterans were twice as likely to be unemployed as White veterans. Many suffered from emotional problems caused by the war. For all Americans the Vietnam War had been a bitter experience. For Blacks, with many of their own problems still unsolved, it was especially cruel.

# Understanding What You Have Read

A. Write the name of the person next to the sentence that identifies him.

Lyndon B. Johnson          Richard Nixon
Robert Kennedy             Martin Luther King, Jr.

_____ 1. He sent the first U. S. combat troops to Vietnam.

_____ 2. He was killed while running for the nomination for president.

_____ 3. He broke with President Johnson and opposed the war.

_____ 4. He took steps to withdraw American forces from the war.

B. In each of the sentences that follow, the underlined word or words make the sentence true or false. If the sentence is true, write **T** in the blank before it. If it is false, write the word or words that make it true.

_____ 1. In Vietnam, Blacks had a <u>lower</u> rate of casualties than Whites.

_____ 2. Black leaders did not want to offend President Johnson because he had <u>favored</u> civil rights.

_____ 3. Dr. Martin Luther King, Jr., felt the war was costing <u>too much</u> in money and men.

_____ 4. Returning Vietnam veterans were <u>honored and rewarded</u>.

## Building Geography Skills

Study the map on this page. Then answer the questions.

1. Which two countries on the main map were communist before 1965? _____

_____

2. Which countries are communist today?

_____

_____

3. The Mekong River runs through parts of which countries? _____

_____

_____

4. How far is Hanoi from Saigon, now called Ho Chi Minh City? _____

**The War in Vietnam**

0    100  Miles
0    100 Kilometers

USSR
China
Alaska
PACIFIC OCEAN
USA
area shown in main map

CHINA

NORTH VIETNAM
BURMA
Hanoi ★  Haiphong
GULF OF TONKIN
HAINAN (CHINA)
DMZ (demilitarized zone)
Vientiane ★
Khe Sanh  Hué
Danang
THAILAND
Mekong River
Pleiku
Bangkok ★
CAMBODIA
SOUTH VIETNAM
GULF OF SIAM
Phnom Penh ★
Camranh bay
Saigon (now Ho Chi Minh City)
Mekong Delta
SOUTH CHINA SEA

- - - national boundaries
★ capitals
▨ Communist before 1965
▨ Communist today
Note: North and South Vietnam were united in 1975 as Vietnam

## Spotlight on People

**Muhammad Ali.** In 1967, the heavyweight champion of the world, Muhammad Ali, was called for induction into the United States Army. He refused to be inducted. He said he had no quarrel with the communists in Vietnam. Besides, he said, serving in the army would conflict with his beliefs as a Muslim. The boxing commission did what no opponent in the boxing ring could do. It took away Ali's title and stopped him from fighting. Ali's refusal to serve was typical of his character. He was independent and outspoken. He had as his personal slogan the boast, "I am the greatest."

Muhammad Ali's original name was Cassius Marcellus Clay. He was born in 1942 in Louisville, Kentucky. He followed the accepted path for Black athletes. He was an outstanding amateur boxer, winning 180 fights. At the 1960 Olympics, he won the gold medal for light-heavyweights. A group of White Louisville businessmen backed his career as a professional boxer. Four years later, in 1964, he fought the champion, Charles "Sonny" Liston.

Clay scored a victory over Liston, to the surprise of the boxing world. Another surprise was in store. The day after his victory, Clay announced that he had joined the Nation of Islam. He took the Islamic name, Muhammad Ali. After Ali refused to be drafted into the army in 1967, the government tried to jail him. He appealed his decision to the Supreme Court and won. But he had to fight in the ring to regain the title that had been taken from him. He lost his first title fight, against Joe Frazier, in 1971. He finally defeated George Foreman in 1974 in Zaire to become champion again.

Ali lost the title in a 1978 bout with Leon Spinks, but he won a rematch later that year. He thus was the only man to win the heavyweight title three times. Now everyone agreed that he was right in calling himself "The Greatest."

## Recalling the Facts

Choose each correct answer and write the letter in the space provided.

_____ 1. When Ali refused to be drafted
    a. he kept his title.
    b. the government gave him another job.
    c. he lost his title.

_____ 2. Before Ali beat Sonny Liston,
    a. he had won only a few fights.
    b. he was called Cassius Clay.
    c. he was a well-known Black Muslim.

_____ 3. When Ali won his case in the Supreme Court,
    a. the boxing commission gave him back his title.
    b. the government paid for his losses.
    c. he still had to fight to regain his title.

_____ 4. Ali won the title for the second time when he defeated
    a. George Foreman.
    b. Leon Spinks.
    c. Joe Frazier.

_____ 5. After Ali won the title from Sonny Liston, he
    a. announced that he had joined the Nation of Islam.
    b. said he was "the Greatest."
    c. appealed his sentence to the Supreme Court.

# Using Primary Sources

**A Black Soldier in Vietnam.** Emanuel J. Holloman, a Black soldier, was in Vietnam for two tours of duty. In training, he studied the Vietnamese language. He was a translator for the U. S. army. Here he writes of his experiences in Vietnam.

Black people seemed to get along better with the Vietnamese, even though they fought the Communists harder than the White GIs. Two or three of the NVAs [North Vietnamese Army soldiers] I interrogated [questioned] told me they knew when Black soldiers were in action, because they would throw everything they could get their hands on—grenades, tear gas, anything. They feared the Black soldier more than the White soldier, because the Black soldier fought more fiercely. . . .

But I think Blacks got along better with the Vietnamese people because they knew the hardships the Vietnamese went through. The majority of the [American soldiers] who came over there looked down on the Vietnamese. They considered them ragged, poor, stupid. They just didn't respect them. I could understand poverty. I had five brothers and three sisters. My mother worked, still works, in an old folks' home. . . . My father works in a garage in New York. . . . I had to leave school after the eighth grade to work in North Carolina.

Anything Blacks got from the Vietnamese, they would pay for. You hardly didn't find a Black cursing a Vietnamese. And a Black would try to learn some of the words. And try to learn a few of their customs. . . .

If nobody talked to them first, a Vietnamese would warm right up to a Black person even if he had never seen one. I remember I was in the 94th Evac hospital in Long Binh, and this Montagnard girl, about thirteen, had been shot. Her jaw was broken. She didn't speak. She started crying. The first person she grabbed was me. She wouldn't let anybody feed her but me. I sat with her all night holding her hand. Believe me, it surprised me. I took care of her for four days.

1. Why does Holloman think Blacks got on better with Vietnamese people? _____

   _____

2. What did North Vietnamese soldiers think of Black Americans? _____

   _____

## CHAPTER REVIEW: CRITICAL THINKING

Some Blacks felt that they should oppose a war against a third-world country like Vietnam. A third-world country is one that is in need of economic development. Many of the Black nations of Africa are third-world countries.

1. How did this view affect the way Blacks served in Vietnam? _____

   _____

2. A young man could avoid being drafted into the armed forces if he was a college student.

   Why do you think this helped Whites more than Blacks during the Vietnam War? _____

   _____

# Chapter 16 LIMITS ON SOCIAL JUSTICE

**AIM: What happened to the civil rights movement in the 1970s?**

1. In the late 1960s, Blacks won many civil rights. The Jim Crow laws were struck down. Blacks won the right to vote and to use public facilities. But it would take time for these rights to affect all areas of daily life. In the northern cities, housing patterns and custom still separated Blacks and Whites. Legally, Blacks had equal opportunities. The great need now was to turn opportunity into real equality.

2. Segregation was illegal. But it was now necessary to pass laws to integrate schools, jobs, and neighborhoods. Many Blacks lived in poor inner-city neighborhoods. Their schools were nearly all Black. The schools often were overcrowded, with inferior equipment and unhappy teachers. One way to change this situation was by busing students to schools in other neighborhoods. The purpose was to bring about racial balance in the schools. Many White people opposed busing. Busing caused bitter conflicts in some northern cities.

3. In 1964, President Lyndon B. Johnson had declared a War on Poverty. The government started social programs to help the poor. Programs provided job training for young people and help for pre-school children. The government made loans to farm cooperatives and small businesses. The **Medicaid** program paid for health care for the poor. However, after Richard Nixon became president in 1969, social programs were cut back. Nixon's advisers did not want to encourage "unrealistic expectations" among Blacks. Some people felt this meant that the concerns of Blacks would be ignored.

4. A new kind of way of achieving equality was started in the 1970s. This was **affirmative action**. Under affirmative action, employers were required to make special efforts to locate and hire Black employees. Schools were to try to find Black teachers and students. The purpose was to give Blacks the jobs and other opportunities they would have had if they had not been discriminated against. People argued over how affirmative action should work. Many White Americans felt threatened by it. They thought it would take jobs away from them and give them to Blacks. Some said affirmative action was racism that was applied against Whites. Blacks did gain many jobs under affirmative action programs. Many Black students entered colleges under affirmative action. Some people questioned whether affirmative action was constitutional and brought cases involving it before the Supreme Court. In general, the court has ruled that affirmative action is not unconstitutional.

5. In 1976, Jimmy Carter, a Georgian, was elected president. Most Blacks voted for him and helped him win the election. He named more Blacks to high posts in his administration than any earlier president. He also named many Black federal judges. One of them was Amalya Kearse, whom he named an appeals court judge in 1979. Carter's foreign policy favored African nations. Blacks felt Carter was sympathetic to supporting industrial and economic development in Africa.

▲ Busing students to schools in other neighborhoods was one way of bringing about racial balance in schools.

# Understanding What You Have Read

A. Next to each name or term in Column A, place the letter of the item in column B that explains it.

**Column A**

_____ 1. War on Poverty

_____ 2. neglect of Black needs

_____ 3. busing

_____ 4. Jimmy Carter

_____ 5. affirmative action

**Column B**

a. sending students to schools outside their own neighborhoods to bring about racial balance

b. President Johnson's programs to help the poor

c. President Nixon's policy toward Blacks

d. program to provide more jobs for Blacks

e. the president who named the most Blacks to high posts

B. In each of the sentences that follow, the underlined word makes the sentence true or false. If the sentence is true, write **T** in the blank before it. If it is false, write the word or words that make it true.

_____ 1. President Nixon <u>increased</u> aid for the poor.

_____ 2. Schools in the inner cities were often <u>better</u> than those in other neighborhoods.

_____ 3. Some Whites thought <u>affirmative action</u> took jobs away from them.

_____ 4. <u>All</u> of the War on Poverty programs were effective.

## Building Graph Skills

Study the graph. Then answer the questions.

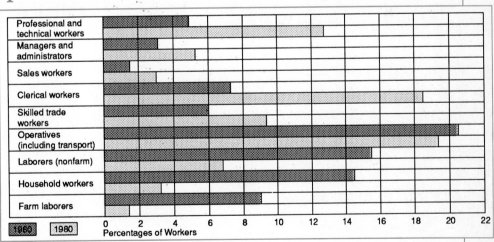

1. In what four types of jobs did the percentage of Black workers *decrease* from 1960 to 1980? _____

2. In what five types of jobs did the percentage of Black workers *increase* from 1960 to 1980? _____

3. What do these statistics tell you about the changes in Black employment? _____ _____

# Spotlight on People

**Barbara Jordan.** Barbara Jordan was born in Houston, Texas, in 1936. "We were poor," Barbara Jordan has said of her childhood, "but so was everyone around us, so we did not notice it." She earned straight A's in school. As she has said, she "wanted to become something unusual." In high school, Jordan heard a Career Day talk by Edith Sampson, a Black lawyer from Chicago. Jordan decided that she too would be a lawyer.

She earned a law degree at Boston University in 1959. Back in Houston, she set up a law office in her parents' house. She helped to win votes for John F. Kennedy in the presidential election of 1960. Two years later, she ran for office herself. Her bid for the Texas House of Representatives failed, but she got 46,000 votes. She said, "I figured anybody who could get 46,000 people to vote for them should keep on trying." In 1966, she won election to the Texas State Senate. She was the first Black to serve there since 1883. She earned respect for her stand in favor of workers and the poor.

Jordan won election to the United States Congress in 1972. She was the first Black woman from the South to be elected to Congress. She became a member of the House Judiciary Committee. In 1974, the committee had to consider whether President Nixon should be impeached, or accused of misconduct, for his part in the Watergate scandal. Only once before, in 1868, had the House Judiciary Committee considered whether to impeach a president. The president in 1868 was Andrew Johnson.

Millions of Americans watched the committee's hearings on television. Many viewers were impressed by the Black Congresswoman's questions and remarks. One news reporter called Barbara Jordan "the best mind on the committee." When the committee approved charges against President Nixon, he resigned. Jordan seemed on the way to a brilliant career. Many were disappointed when she did not run for re-election in 1976. The reason was poor health. She returned to Houston, where she teaches at the University of Texas.

## Recalling the Facts

Choose each correct answer and write the letter in the space provided.

_____ 1. Jordan decided to be a lawyer because
    a. she heard a talk by a Black woman lawyer.
    b. her father was a lawyer.
    c. she supported John Kennedy.

_____ 2. The first time she ran for office, Jordan
    a. was elected to the Texas Senate.
    b. was elected to the United States Congress.
    c. lost, but many people voted for her.

_____ 3. In Congress, Jordan
    a. served as head of the House Judiciary Committee.
    b. served as a member of the House Judiciary Committee.
    c. was committee chairperson.

_____ 4. Jordan became nationally known when she
    a. ran for president.
    b. wrote a famous book.
    c. was seen on the televised impeachment hearings.

_____ 5. Today, Jordan is
    a. still a member of Congress.
    b. a U. S. Senator.
    c. a teacher.

# The Arts and Technology

**Recording.** The most successful Afro-American business in 1975 was Motown Industries, a record company. It was started by Berry Gordy, Jr. Born in Detroit, Gordy was from a family that hoped to become middle class. He tried to become a boxer. Then he wrote songs. After serving in the army, Gordy opened a record shop in 1953. He went broke. He took a job at the Ford plant.

During the 1950s, rock and roll became the most popular music in America. Rock developed from the Black rhythm and blues tradition. Many White singers recorded songs that were already hits in the Black community. Black rock stars soon became famous in their own right.

In 1959, Barry Gordy used a $700 loan to start his own record company. He named it "Motown." This was a popular name for Detroit, the home of the auto industry. Motown Records had its first gold record in 1960. It was made by Smokey Robinson and the Miracles. Robinson later became vice-president of the company. Throughout the 1960s and 1970s, Motown had many hits. The distinctive sound of its artists was a

winner. Gordy's record artists included the Supremes, Marvin Gaye, Stevie Wonder, and later the Jackson Five.

▲ Stevie Wonder, the blind musician, was one of the most popular performers who recorded for Motown.

1. How would you summarize Berry Gordy's career? _____

_____

2. From where did rock and roll music develop? _____

_____

## CHAPTER REVIEW: CRITICAL THINKING

Busing of school children and affirmative action as ways of giving Blacks greater opportunities had both supporters and critics.

1. What arguments can you think for and against busing? What other solutions to improving

   inner-city schools can you suggest? _____

_____

2. What arguments can you think of in favor of and against affirmative action? _____

_____

_____

# UNIT 4 REVIEW

## Summary of the Unit

A few of the most important events and facts presented in Unit 4 are listed below. Write these in your notebook and add three more.

1. In 1954, the Supreme Court ruled that segregated schools were illegal. This paved the way for a new era of civil rights.
2. Beginning in the mid-1950s, Blacks began a new protest to win their rights. Dr. Martin Luther King, Jr., led protestors in using non-violent methods.
3. Progress was too slow for many Blacks. Some began to return self-defense or violence with violence.
4. The Vietnam War took attention away from the civil rights movement. Many Blacks served in the armed forces in Vietnam.
5. In the 1970s, busing and affirmative action were used to overcome discrimination.

## Understanding What You Have Read

Choose each answer and write the letter in the space provided.

_____ 1. President Eisenhower sent federal troops to Little Rock, Arkansas
   a. to help the state police there.
   b. to make sure Blacks could go to the Little Rock high school.
   c. to force the state to allow Blacks to vote.

_____ 2. Rosa Parks started a new stage in the civil rights movement when she
   a. refused to leave a lunch counter.
   b. led a march through Birmingham.
   c. would not give up her seat on a bus.

_____ 3. Violence against civil rights protestors
   a. won new sympathy for their cause.
   b. made them give up the fight.
   c. seldom happened.

_____ 4. Dr. Martin Luther King, Jr., believed in non-violence because
   a. he thought Blacks were too weak to overcome Whites.
   b. he wanted the government to help Blacks.
   c. he thought violence was immoral, and the cause of civil rights was moral.

_____ 5. Blacks who served in the Vietnam War
   a. had a higher casualty rate than Whites.
   b. decided to protest by refusing to fight.
   c. usually were not sent into combat.

_____ 6. The president who started a War on Poverty was
   a. Jimmy Carter.
   b. Richard Nixon.
   c. Lyndon Johnson.

## Building Your Vocabulary

Complete each of the sentences below by choosing one of the following words or terms.

        casualty      busing        militant
        sit-in        integration   affirmative action

1. Moving students to other schools to bring about racial balance is called _____.

2. A person wounded or killed in war is called a _____.

3. The practice of occupying seats in a racially segregated place to protest discrimination is called a _____.

4. A person who does not believe in nonviolence to reach a goal is called a _____.

5. A way of improving the employment or educational opportunities of a minority group is called _____.

6. Bringing people of different races together on an equal basis is called _____.

## Developing Ideas and Skills—Using a Timeline

Study the timeline. In each of the sentences that follow, the underlined word, or words, or dates, make the sentence true or false. If the sentence is true, write **T** on the line next to it. If it is false, write the word, words, or dates that make it true.

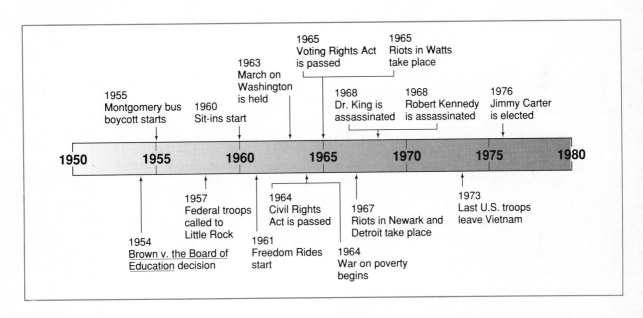

_____ 1. Martin Luther King, Jr., <u>did not</u> live to see the Voting Rights Act passed.

_____ 2. The March on Washington <u>led to</u> the Montgomery bus boycott.

_____ 3. The two civil rights acts passed in this period became law in <u>1964 and 1965</u>.

_____ 4. Dr. King was assassinated <u>12</u> years after the Brown decision.

_____ 5. The War on Poverty began <u>one year</u> after the March on Washington.

## Making History Live

1. Interview a person who took part in the civil rights movement in the 1960s. Then write a report about that person's activities. Include the person's personal feelings about the experience.
2. Find out more about the sit-ins, the Freedom Rides, and other civil rights activities of this time. Write a report on how these actions worked.

# Chapter 17 A NEW LEADERSHIP ROLE

**AIM: What gains have Black Americans made in political leadership?**

1. "We are ... in the first generation of Black success after 20 generations in this country." This is how Eleanor Holmes Norton, a Black lawyer, sees political progress for today's Black Americans. Several factors have contributed to Black success. The Voting Rights Act of 1965 made sure Blacks could vote. That, and voter registration drives held by civil rights workers, were the keys to Black political power. In 1988, there were almost 7,000 Black Americans in elected offices. In 1955, there were fewer than 100.

2. Today, a number of cities with large Black populations have Black mayors. The first was Carl Stokes. He was elected mayor of Cleveland in 1967. Black mayors came to office in other large cities in the late 1960s through the 1980s. Coleman Young became mayor of Detroit. Thomas Bradley became the mayor of Los Angeles in 1973. Black women have also won the office of mayor. In 1988, 48 Black women were mayors of cities across the na-tion. Carrie Saxon Perry was elected mayor of Hartford, Connecticut, in 1987. With her victory, Perry became the first Black female mayor of a major northeastern city.

3. Political change for Blacks has been greatest in the South. Today, Blacks serve in the legislatures of states where they could not even vote 30 years ago. Alyce G. Clarke is one such Black legislator. She was elected to Mississippi's House of Representatives in 1985. She was the first Black woman to serve in that state's legislature.

4. In the United States Senate, Edward W. Brooke was elected senator from Massachusetts in 1966. He was the first Black senator since Reconstruction. Brook served in the Senate for 12 years. As of 1988, there were no Blacks in the Senate. However, there were 23 Blacks in the House of Representatives. Several hold important committee posts. For example, William Gray of Pennsylvania chaired the Budget Committee. This committee controls the way Congress spends the nation's tax money. In the early 1970s, the Black members of Congress formed a group called the Congressional Black Caucus. They discuss issues of importance to Blacks.

5. Blacks have also been named to posts in the national government. In 1967, President Lyndon B. Johnson appointed Thurgood Marshall to the United States Supreme Court. Marshall is the only Black ever to sit on the country's highest court. Johnson also named Robert Weaver as Secretary of Housing and Urban Development. He was the first Black to hold a cabinet post.

6. Black women have played important roles in national politics. In 1968, Shirley Chisholm of New York City was the first Black woman ever elected to Congress. In 1972, she was the first Black to run for President. In the 1970s, Barbara Jordan of Texas was one of the best-known members of Congress. She was on the committee that brought charges against President Nixon in the Watergate affair.

▲ Carrie Saxon Perry is mayor of Hartford, Connecticut.

## Understanding What You Have Read

A. Write the name of the person next to the statement he or she might have made.

Shirley Chisholm    Carl Stokes       Barbara Jordan
Edward Brooke     Thurgood Marshall

_____ 1. I was the first Black to be named to the Supreme Court.

_____ 2. I was the first Black senator since Reconstruction.

_____ 3. I was a member of the committee that brought charges against President Nixon in the Watergate affair.

_____ 4. I was the first Black to run for president.

_____ 5. I was the first Black elected mayor of a big city.

B. In each of the following sentences, the underlined word or words make the sentence true or false. If the sentence is true, write **T** in the blank before it. If it is false, write the word or words that would make it true.

_____ 1. As of 1988, there were 23 Black members of the United States <u>Senate</u>.

_____ 2. Today, Blacks <u>serve in the legislatures</u> of many southern states.

_____ 3. President <u>John F. Kennedy</u> named the first Black to a cabinet post.

_____ 4. In 1987, <u>Carrie Saxon Perry</u> was elected mayor of Hartford, Connecticut.

## Building Geography Skills

Study the map. Then answer the questions.

1. What city on the map has the greatest percentage of Blacks?

   _____

2. What city on the map has the smallest percentage of Blacks?

   _____

3. How many cities have a Black population of over 60 percent?

   _____

4. Where are the cities with over 60 percent Black population located?

   _____

   _____

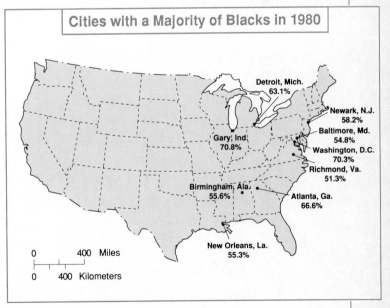

**Cities with a Majority of Blacks in 1980**

Detroit, Mich. 63.1%
Newark, N.J. 58.2%
Baltimore, Md. 54.8%
Gary, Ind. 70.8%
Washington, D.C. 70.3%
Richmond, Va. 51.3%
Birmingham, Ala. 55.6%
Atlanta, Ga. 66.6%
New Orleans, La. 55.3%

0    400 Miles
0    400 Kilometers

**Jesse Jackson.** In the 1980s, Jesse Jackson became the country's most important Black political leader. He first ran for president in 1984. At that time, people doubted he would win much support. Jackson silenced the doubters by winning primaries in several states. No Black man had ever done this. Four years later, when Jackson ran again, he had a better organization. This time, he attracted large numbers of White votes.

Jackson was born in Greenville, South Carolina, in 1941 and went to high school there. He graduated from North Carolina A & T University and studied at Chicago Theological Seminary. He became a Baptist minister in 1968. Jackson worked closely with Dr. Martin Luther King, Jr.

Dr. King chose Jackson to start a group of Black business and religious leaders in Chicago. The group began a program called Operation Breadbasket. The purpose of Operation Breadbasket was to develop greater job opportunities for Blacks. The project was successful in Chicago and spread to other cities.

In 1971, Jackson began another group called People United to Save Humanity (PUSH). PUSH encouraged large businesses to give jobs to Blacks. The group also started education and job training programs.

After Jackson lost his first race for president, he worked to register new voters. Two million more Democratic voters registered between 1984 and 1986. Most of them were Blacks. Jackson often speaks at schools in the inner city. He tells students to avoid drugs and stay in school.

In the presidential election of 1988, Jackson finished first or second in many state primaries. His appeal was seen in both North and South. Jackson is a powerful political leader. His 1988 campaign showed that a Black candidate could appeal to all voters. It also showed that many American voters cared more about issues than the color of a candidate's skin.

## Recalling the Facts

Choose each correct answer and write the letter in the space provided.

_____ 1. PUSH started
   a. voter registration programs.
   b. new churches.
   c. job training and education programs.

_____ 2. Jackson worked closely with
   a. White political leaders.
   b. Dr. Martin Luther King, Jr.
   c. Shirley Chisholm.

_____ 3. Operation Breadbasket tried to
   a. win votes for Black leaders.
   b. register new voters.
   c. develop greater job opportunities for Blacks.

_____ 4. In 1984, Jesse Jackson
   a. won primary elections in several states.
   b. attracted large numbers of White votes.
   c. did not attract much support from Whites or Blacks.

_____ 5. After his defeat in 1984, Jackson
   a. did not run again for president.
   b. refused to help the Democratic party.
   c. worked to register new voters.

# The Arts and Technology

**The Dance.** Dancing has been an important part of Black life since the days of slavery. In this century, many Blacks have been important in the world of dance. Katherine Dunham was the first dancer to bring the world of Black dance to the American public. She traveled and studied dances from all parts of the Black world. Dunham absorbed the styles of Africa, the Caribbean, and the United States, and wove a new kind of dance. She also created one of the first professional Black dance companies. Dunham staged Broadway shows and appeared in movies. Perhaps her greatest work is as a teacher. She has inspired many Black dancers. One of them is Alvin Ailey, founder of the Alvin Ailey Dance Company.

In the 1950s, Arthur Mitchell was one of the most popular dancers of the New York City Ballet. Mitchell studied at the School of American Ballet and was the first Black to join the New York City Ballet. Later, he became a principal dancer of the company. Mitchell was an outstanding classical dancer and created many roles. In 1968, Mitchell founded the Dance Theatre of Harlem. His goal was to teach children the art of dance. Mitchell wanted to help Blacks realize they can have a career in the classical arts. One of the most interesting stagings in the company's history is its all-Black version of the ballet *Giselle*. The Dance Theatre of Harlem's staging sets the ballet in the Louisiana bayou. The company has performed all over the world, including the Soviet Union. Mitchell's choreography, or dance design, has brought him world fame. Like Katherine Dunham, Arthur Mitchell has created a special kind of dance.

▲ Arthur Mitchell enjoys working with the students of the Dance Theatre of Harlem.

1. Katherine Dunham combined dance styles from _____

2. Arthur Mitchell was the first Black to join _____

3. The purpose of the Dance Theatre of Harlem is _____

## CHAPTER REVIEW: CRITICAL THINKING

1. The fact that many Blacks lived in cities in the 1960s, 1970s, and 1980s helped them elect mayors and other public officials. Then, as now, they make up a sizable group of voters. Thus far, there are no states in which Blacks are governors. Give one reason why you think

   this is so. _____

   _____

2. Why, do you think, are attitudes toward Black political candidates changing? _____

   _____

   _____

# Chapter 18

# BLACKS AND THE ECONOMY

**AIM: How well have Blacks managed in today's economy?**

1. As the United States has moved closer to racial equality, many Blacks have taken advantage of new opportunities in the economy. There is now a sizable Black middle class. Its members earn comfortable incomes in professional, managerial, and technical jobs.

2. Several factors have helped Blacks move forward in the economic life of the country. More Blacks have gone on to earn college and advanced degrees. Programs of businesses have brought Blacks into new kinds of jobs. The Equal Employment Opportunity Commission (EEOC) of the federal government has seen to it that businesses hire workers without regard to race, religion, or sex. The government has also helped to fund child care centers.

▲ One Black woman who has risen to a top executive position at a major corporation is Toni Fay. She works for Time, Inc.

This kind of assistance allows many mothers to stay in the work force.

3. On the other hand, large numbers of other Blacks still suffer from poverty. Conditions in many inner cities where Blacks live are worse now than they were in the riot-torn 1960s. In many cities, Blacks live in the poorest, most run-down neighborhoods. Many buildings are in a state of decay. Drug pushers and the crime that comes from drug dealing terrorize Black families. Some families are headed by single mothers on welfare. Teenagers who have dropped out of school have limited skills or training. They have great difficulty finding work. Homeless men and women live in shelters or on the streets.

4. Changes in the economy have hurt the Black working class. Blacks have long worked in heavy industries such as steel and automobile manufacturing. Since the 1970s, these industries have been hard hit by foreign competition. Many factories have closed in industrial cities where Blacks lived. Workers have been laid off. Another change in the American economy is the growth of **services** at the expense of manufacturing. Service work includes computer operation and office work in general. Repair work, hotel operation, and the professions are other kinds of service work. Most jobs like these require training. Black workers as well as White workers who have lost jobs in manufacturing have had to be retrained to find jobs in today's business world.

5. At the same time, some Blacks have been successful in starting new businesses. One of the largest Black-owned businesses in the United States is the Philadelphia Coca-Cola Bottling Company. It is owned by basketball star Julius ("Dr. J") Erving and J. Bruce Llewellyn. Former fashion model Naomi Sims started a successful cosmetics business. Her products are sold in department stores across the nation. Carol Coe heads her own law firm and owns a petroleum company in Kansas. Black business people are contributing to the nation's economic wealth and to the self-esteem of all Blacks.

A. Fill in the blank with the term that best completes each sentence.

middle class     heavy industries     retrain     professional     college

_____ 1. New opportunities in the economy have led to the growth of a sizable Black _____.

_____ 2. Today, Blacks earn comfortable salaries in managerial, technical, and _____ jobs.

_____ 3. Blacks have moved forward in the economy because more Black men and women have earned _____ degrees.

_____ 4. Members of the Black and White working class have been hurt by a decline in the number of _____ in the United States.

_____ 5. Members of the working class have had to _____ in order to find new jobs in today's business world.

B. In each of the following sentences, the underlined word or words make the sentence true or false. If the sentence is true, write **T** in the blank before it. If it is false, write the word or words that would make it true.

_____ 1. Conditions in many inner cities are <u>worse</u> now than they were in the riot-torn 1960s.

_____ 2. The Black working class has been hurt by a <u>rise</u> in the number of heavy industries in the United States.

_____ 3. Even as the economy changes, some Black businesspeople have been <u>successful</u> in starting new businesses.

_____ 4. Lack of adequate housing is one of the problems of <u>middle-class life</u>.

## Building Graph Skills

Review the graphs. Then answer the questions.

1. The percentage of Blacks who completed high school in 1987 was _____.

2. The percentage of Blacks who completed four years of college went _____ between 1978 and 1987.

3. The percentage of Blacks who complete more than four years of college went _____ between 1978 and 1987.

### Black Education

Percentage of Blacks 25–29 years old in March of each year who completed high school, college, or graduate study. Figure for 1987 is estimated.

**High School**
55.8  '68
77.3  '78
83.3  '87

**College 4 years**
4.7  '68
8.3  '78
9.1  '87

**College 5 or more years**
0.7  '68
3.5  '78
2.3  '87

Source: Education Department

79 ▶

**Guion S. Bluford, Jr.** One of the Black Americans whose education brought him success was the astronaut Guion Bluford, Jr. When the space shuttle *Challenger* blasted into space in August 1983, Bluford was aboard.

Bluford was the oldest of three sons. His father was an engineer and inventor. His mother taught in the Philadelphia public schools. As a boy, he built model airplanes and became interested in flying. While he was in high school, the first Americans went into space. "Guy" Bluford decided to be an aerospace engineer. This is a scientist who studies ways of flying into outer space.

Bluford's brother recalled that school was not easy for Guy. "He just had to work harder than the rest of us. He put in very long hours." In fact, a high-school counselor told his family that Guy should not try for college. His family encouraged Guy in his goal and he was accepted at Penn State University in 1960. Guy was the only Black student in the engineering school there.

Upon graduation from college, Bluford went into the U.S. Air Force. He earned his "wings" as a pilot and was sent to Vietnam. He flew 144 combat missions during the war and won more than a dozen medals.

Bluford still wanted to fly higher. To get there, he had to continue his studies. He earned a Ph.D. degree in aerospace engineering. In 1978, he was one of 35 astronaut trainees picked from 10,000 who applied. His flight in space lasted more than six days. His scientific training helped him carry out several important experiments.

Bluford played down the fact that he was the first Black American in space. But his success made him a role model for others. He once told a group of students: "It's very important to set high goals for yourself and realize that if you work hard you will get them. I want you to be the future astronauts flying in space with me."

## Recalling the Facts

Choose each correct answer and write the letter in the space provided.

_____ 1. Guion Bluford, Jr., first went into space in
    a. 1981.   b. 1983.   c. 1984.

_____ 2. In high school, Bluford
    a. found his studies easy.
    b. wanted to drop out.
    c. was not encouraged to try for college.

_____ 3. During the Vietnam War, Bluford was
    a. studying to be an astronaut.
    b. a pilot who won many medals.
    c. still a child.

_____ 4. Bluford's scientific training
    a. was useful in space.
    b. stopped after he entered the Air Force.
    c. was not important to becoming an astronaut.

_____ 5. Bluford tells young people
    a. to set high goals for themselves.
    b. they should not go into space.
    c. that they should not take part in wars.

# The Arts and Technology

**Black Scientists Today.** Scientists need years of training in a university. Before the civil-rights movement, few Blacks were able to get this kind of advanced education. The highest college degree is called a doctorate. About 95 percent of American Blacks who ever received a science doctorate are living today. The following are just a few Black scientists who have risen to the top of their fields.

• David H. Blackwell is a famous mathematician. He earned his doctorate from the University of Illinois in 1941. In 1965, he became the first Black member of the National Academy of Sciences.

• Henry Aaron Hill received his doctorate in chemistry from the Massachusetts Institute of Technology in 1942. In 1972, he was the first Black to be nominated for president of the American Chemical Society.

• Samuel M. Nabrit received his doctorate from Brown University in 1932. He became president of Texas Southern University in 1955. (His brother James, a lawyer, was president of Howard University at the same time.) Samuel Nabrit was the first Black member of the United States Atomic Energy Commission in 1966–1967.

• Paul B. Cornely received a doctorate in public health from the University of Michigan in 1934. In 1969–1970 he was president of the American Public Health Association.

▲ Dr. Jane C. Wright did important cancer research.

• Jane C. Wright received an M.D. degree from New York Medical College in 1945. She did important research in cancer as director of the Harlem Hospital Cancer Research Foundation. In 1965, Wright received the Distinguished Service Award of the American Medical Association.

• J. Ernest Wilkins received his doctorate from the University of Chicago in 1942. He worked on the Manhattan Project that developed the first atomic bomb.

• Ronald McNair was one of the Black astronaut trainees chosen in 1978 with Guion Bluford, Jr. McNair was a brilliant laser scientist and a jazz musician. On his first trip into space in 1986, the space shuttle exploded. McNair and the other astronauts aboard were killed.

1. The highest degree you can earn in a university is called a _____.

2. The first Black member of the Atomic Energy Commission was _____.

3. _____ received the Distinguished Service Award of the American Medical Association in 1965.

## CHAPTER REVIEW: CRITICAL THINKING

1. Some people have argued that social welfare programs encourage people not to work. Thus, they keep people from ever moving above the poverty level. Do you agree or disagree? Explain your answer. _____

_____

2. Explain the connection between the rise in Blacks attending college and the rise in Black incomes. _____

_____

# 19 EXCELLENCE IN THE ARTS AND SPORTS

**AIM: What are the achievements of Black Americans in the arts and sports?**

1. Many new Black writers have appeared in recent years. Alice Walker, Maya Angelou, and Toni Morrison have written best-selling novels. Rita Dove won the Pulitzer Prize for poetry in 1987 for her work titled *Thomas and Beulah*. This was based on the story of her grandparents' lives.

2. Black artists have a bigger audience than ever. Painters such as Romare Beardon and Lois Maillou Jones have earned high praise for their work. John Wilson has gained fame as a sculptor. His bust of Dr. Martin Luther King, Jr., is in the United States capitol building in Washington, D.C.

3. Today, Black Americans play in almost all the major league sports. It was not always so. Discrimination kept them out in the past. Other reasons also contributed to their absence. Professional sports like football and basketball took their players from colleges. This left out most Black young people. The situation changed, however, as colleges opened their doors to Blacks. More Black players could show their talents on college teams and make it to professional teams.

4. As in the society as a whole, some prejudice remains. In football, Black college quarterbacks were usually moved to other positions when they joined the pros. Times changed however, and in 1988 Doug Williams of the Washington Redskins was the first Black quarterback to lead his team to victory in the Super Bowl. Despite the odds, many Black athletes have achieved in sports that were limited to White upper and middle class youth. In the late 1950s Althea Gibson won the English and American tennis championships. She was the first major Black tennis player. In 1988, Debi Thomas won a bronze medal for figure skating at the Olympic games in Calgary, Canada.

5. Show business is another field in which Blacks have risen to the top. One of the most popular movie stars in the United States is Eddie Murphy. His movie *Beverly Hills Cop* made more than $100 million in 1984. The comic talents of Whoopi Goldberg have won her millions of fans. Bill Cosby produces and stars in the most popular series in TV history, *The Cosby Show*.

6. In popular music, songwriters and singers Ray Charles and Stevie Wonder head a list of superstars. Their songs are known all over the world. Another successful singer of the late 1980s is Whitney Houston. She won a 1985 Grammy Award for best female pop vocalist. The biggest superstar of the 1980s was Michael Jackson. Music fans all over the world know Michael Jackson from his music tours and rock videos. His songs made *Thriller* the best-selling album of 1983.

▲ Bill Cosby is known as an entertainer and writer. He also holds a doctorate degree.

## Understanding What You Have Read

A. Write the name of the person next to the statement he or she might have made.

Rita Dove          Doug Williams          Eddie Murphy
Whitney Houston          Michael Jackson

_____ 1. In 1985 I won the Grammy Award for best female pop vocalist.

_____ 2. I was the first Black quarterback to lead a team to victory in the Super Bowl.

_____ 3. My work *Thomas and Beulah* won the Pulitzer Prize for poetry in 1987.

_____ 4. My album *Thriller* was the best-seller of 1983.

_____ 5. I was the star of *Beverly Hills Cop*, a movie that made over $100 million.

B. In each of the sentences that follow, the underlined word or words make the sentence true or false. If the sentence is true, write **T** in the blank before it. If it is false, write the word or words that would make it true.

_____ 1. Rita Dove based *Thomas and Beulah* on her <u>parents</u>.

_____ 2. Ray Charles is a world famous <u>actor</u>.

_____ 3. When more Blacks began to attend college, <u>fewer</u> Blacks became pro basketball and football players.

_____ 4. Althea Gibson was a star in <u>ice skating.</u>

## Building Chart Skills

Read the following chart of Black Pulitzer Prize winners and answer the questions. The Pulitzer prizes are awarded every year for outstanding work in various fields such as poetry, fiction writing, history, and drama.

**Some Black Pulitzer Prize Winners**

| Winner | Type of Work | Year |
|---|---|---|
| Gwendolyn Brooks | poetry, *Annie Allen* | 1950 |
| Alex Haley | special category, *Roots* | 1977 |
| Alice Walker | fiction, *The Color Purple* | 1983 |
| Rita Dove | poetry, *Thomas and Beulah* | 1987 |
| August Wilson | drama, *Fences* | 1987 |
| Toni Morrison | fiction, *Beloved* | 1987 |

1. Who was the author of *Roots*? _____

2. Who won the prize for fiction in 1987? _____

3. Gwendolyn Brooks, the poet, won the Pulitzer Prize in _____.

4. The play *Fences* tells of the relationship between a Black father and son. The author is

_____.

**Alice Walker.** Alice Walker's poems and novels have come out of her experiences in life. Her first book, called *Once*, included poems about Africa, love, and the civil rights movement. Walker grew up at a time when the movement was beginning. She took part in demonstrations in Atlanta in the 1960s. She spent the summer of 1964 in Africa. Afterward, she wrote the poems in *Once*. The book made her one of the best known of today's Black writers.

Alice Walker's father was a Georgia sharecropper. Her mother worked as a maid. When Alice won a scholarship to college, her parents did not even have the money to pay her travel expenses. Neighbors raised the money it cost for the bus ride to college.

After graduation, Alice married a White lawyer who shared her concern for civil rights. They moved to Mississippi, where Alice worked to register voters. All the while she was teaching in Black colleges. She wrote her first novel while in Mississippi.

Walker became active in women's rights and the anti-war movement in the 1960s and 1970s. Her next novel seemed to draw from her own life. It described the challenges of being a Black and a woman. It was poorly received by the critics. Walker was not discouraged. She continued to write about Black women.

Her third novel, *The Color Purple*, was a great success. Written in letter form, it told the story of Celie, a poor southern Black woman. It was a best-seller and was made into a movie. Walker said of the characters in *The Color Purple*: "I'm really paying homage [respect] to people I love, the people who are thought to be dumb and backward, but who were the ones who first taught me to see beauty."

## Recalling the Facts

Choose each correct answer and write the letter in the space provided.

_____ 1. Alice Walker's first book of poems
   a. made her famous.
   b. took a long time to write.
   c. was made into a movie.

_____ 2. Walker got the ideas for her poems
   a. from reading.
   b. from listening to her mother's stories.
   c. from her own experiences.

_____ 3. After graduating from college, Walker
   a. moved to Africa.
   b. moved to Mississippi.
   c. lost interest in civil rights.

_____ 4. *The Color Purple* is about
   a. a poor southern Black woman.
   b. a wealthy Black woman.
   c. women in Africa.

_____ 5. Walker says she
   a. feels sorry for the people she writes about.
   b. has no feeling about the characters in her books.
   c. loves the people she writes about.

# The Arts and Technology

**Television.** In the early years of television, very few shows had Black characters or stars. In the 1950s, the most popular show with Black entertainers was *Amos and Andy*. The NAACP attacked the show because it portrayed Black Americans as being lazy and clownish. White audiences and television producers were not ready for a show with a serious Black character.

Thirty years later, one of the most popular and successful television stars is Oprah Winfrey. Since 1984, Winfrey has been the star of her own daytime talk show. It is one of the most watched shows in the United States. In 1987, she won an Emmy award for the best talk show host.

While in college Winfrey was hired to become Nashville's first Black woman newscaster on the TV evening news. Upon graduation, Winfrey took a job in Baltimore, Maryland, as the cohost of a morning talk show. Viewers loved Winfrey's free-wheeling discussions, but more than that, they were drawn to her down-to-earth sense of humor and honesty.

Success took Winfrey to Chicago in 1984 and her **very** own talk show. She continued to talk about tough social issues. One of her goals was to take her show to South Africa—a nation where racial problems are deep. As Winfrey once said about her talk show: "We go to the heart of the matter."

Another Black woman who has succeeded in television is Charlayne Hunter-

▲ Oprah Winfrey has become one of television's most popular talk show hosts.

Gault. She is a regular correspondent of the MacNeil/Lehrer News Hour on the Public Broadcasting System. Hunter-Gault was active in the civil rights movement. In 1961, she was one of the first two Black students to enter the University of Georgia. In 1968, she became a reporter for *The New York Times*. She joined the MacNeil/Lehrer show in 1978. Hunter-Gault has broadcast important stories about Blacks. They include one on the poor quality of health care for the poor and the high death rate of infants born to poor Black teenage mothers.

Bernard Shaw, another Black broadcast journalist, is chief Washington anchor for the Cable News Network. A **journalist** is a reporter or broadcaster who deals with the news. Shaw is one of many Black journalists who now bring the news to America's millions on television.

1. In the _____, White audiences and television producers were not ready for a show with serious Black characters.

2. In the 1980s, Oprah Winfrey became the star of her own daytime _____.

3. Two of the Black journalists on television are _____.

## CHAPTER REVIEW: CRITICAL THINKING

1. Why do you think the position of quarterback was once reserved for Whites in pro football?

_____

2. On *The Cosby Show*, one parent is a doctor and the other a lawyer. Some people have said that *The Cosby Show* is successful because it shows Blacks as Whites would like them to be.

Do you agree or disagree? Explain your answer. _____

# Chapter 20 ACHIEVEMENTS AND CHALLENGES

**AIM: How has life improved for Black Americans? What problems remain to be solved?**

1. "History helps Black people have a sense of pride." These words by Dexter King, son of Dr. Martin Luther King, Jr., remind Americans that Blacks have much of which to be proud. Through more than 300 years of struggle, they have achieved a better life.

2. There are over 29 million Blacks in the United States today. They are the country's largest minority group. Twelve out of every 100 Americans are Black. More than half the Blacks, or over 14 million, still live in the South. Most Blacks live in cities. More Blacks live in New York City than in any other city of the United States. In many cities, such as Atlanta, Georgia; Baltimore, Maryland; Detroit, Michigan; and Washington, D.C., they make up the majority of the population.

3. A high percentage of this large Black

▲ On the anniversary of Dr. Martin Luther King's death, a grown-up shows a child a photograph of the Black leader.

population votes in elections. As a result, Blacks have considerable political power. Blacks hold political office at every level of government. In 1988, there were over 300 Black mayors. Hundreds of Blacks are members of state legislatures. Blacks also serve as judges in state and federal courts.

4. Education is another field where Blacks have made great progress. Blacks are better educated today than ever before. Over one-third of the Black population has completed high school. This is about three times as many as in 1960. Ten out of 100 Blacks have college degrees now, compared with three out of 100 in 1960.

5. With better education, Blacks have made important changes in the kinds of work they do. More than 11 Black men out of 100 and 14 Black women out of 100 are professionals, working as teachers, college professors, doctors, lawyers, and managers. This is five times the number who were professionals in 1940.

6. Blacks hold leading positions in their fields. The head of the United States Military Academy at West Point is Brigadier General Fred A. Gordon, a Black man. The president of the National Education Association, a large teachers' organization, is a Black woman, Mary Hatwood Futrell.

7. Black Americans continue to strive for equality. Black organizations, parents, and teachers are urging Black youths to stay in school so that they can gain the skills and education they need for good jobs and careers. Parents and teachers tell young Blacks it is important for them to have a **role model**. A role model is someone of whom a young person can say, "I want to be like that person."

8. For many Black Americans their hero and role model is Dr. Martin Luther King, Jr. His life showed how the ideals of his people could be put into practice. His "dream" is recognized as the dream of many Americans. King often quoted these words from an old spiritual: "Free at last, free at last. Thank God almighty, I'm free at last."

**A.** Fill in the blank with the term that best completes each sentence.

role model      New York City      judges      skills

_____ 1. More Blacks live in _____ than in any other city of the United States.

_____ 2. Blacks serve as _____ in State and Federal courts.

_____ 3. Teachers urge Black youths to stay in school and gain the education and _____ they need for good jobs.

_____ 4. A _____ is someone who inspires someone else to lead a full, challenging life.

**B.** In each of the following sentences, the underlined word makes the sentence true or false. If the sentence is true, write **T** in the blank before it. If it is false, write in the word or words that make it true.

_____ 1. Through more than 300 years of struggle, Blacks have achieved a <u>better</u> life.

_____ 2. In Washington, D.C., Blacks are a <u>minority</u> of the population.

_____ 3. More than half the Black population of the United States lives in the <u>North</u>.

_____ 4. With better education, Blacks have made <u>few</u> changes in the kinds of work they do.

## Linking Past to Present

Carter Woodson is the father of Black History Month. In 1916, Woodson started the *Journal of Negro History*. Ten years later, in 1926, he began Negro History Week. He chose the second week in February in memory of the birthdays of Abraham Lincoln and Frederick Douglass.

In the 1960s, Black History Week became a regular event in schools and libraries. By 1976, there were so many celebrations and programs that a week was not long enough. That year, Black History Week was extended to a full month. By 1980, February was known as Black History Month across the country.

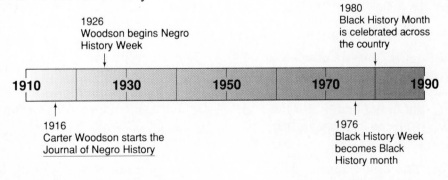

1. The father of Black History Month is _____.

2. When did Negro History Week begin? _____

3. What projects did you take part in this past Black History Month? _____

**Marva Collins.** Not many schoolteachers have had a TV movie made about their lives. Marva Collins is one teacher who has always done things others said couldn't be done.

Marva Collins was born in Monroeville, Alabama. She went to a segregated school. Marva loved to read but Black children could not take books out of the local library. To keep reading, Collins read the Bible and books that her father bought for her. After graduating from Clark College in Atlanta, she taught at a training school for secretaries in Alabama.

In time, Marva Collins moved to Chicago, where she became a substitute in the public schools. She was usually sent to schools in the inner city. Marva challenged her students. She helped them put on scenes from plays and musicals. Some teachers thought this was a waste of time.

To teach the way she wanted, Collins opened her own school. Her husband built a schoolroom in a vacant floor of their apartment building. Collins used books that she found in the trash cans of public schools. She made her students read such classics as *Aesop's Fables*, *Uncle Tom's Cabin*, and *Macbeth*. When she taught math, she told students about ancient Greek mathematicians.

The word soon spread about Collins' school. People were excited about what she was doing. In three years she had 28 students and a waiting list of 175. A Chicago newspaper ran a story about her. A Chicago business leader gave $50,000 to Collins' school when he read the story.

In 1981, CBS made a TV movie of her life. The money from the movie let Marva move her school to a new building.

Schools around the country wanted Marva Collins to show others how to teach. The rock star Prince gave her money to start a teacher training program. Today, Marva Collins is an advisor on education for the federal government. Her first love is her own school, however. Today, her school is larger than ever. She says her secret is to show children the value of education, so they will "want to learn for the sake of learning."

## Recalling the Facts

Choose each correct answer and write the letter in the space provided.

_____ 1. As a girl, Marva Collins read books
   a. from the library.
   b. her father bought for her.
   c. from the Chicago public schools.

_____ 2. Marva Collins started her own school so that she could
   a. earn more money.
   b. teach better students.
   c. teach the way she wanted.

_____ 3. With the money she was paid for the movie of her life, Marva
   a. made her school larger.
   b. moved back to Alabama.
   c. wrote a book.

_____ 4. Today, Marva Collins
   a. is in charge of the Chicago public schools.
   b. advises on education.
   c. has closed her own school.

# Using Primary Sources

The following are letters from Black students. The letters were written during Black History Month. Students were asked to describe the progress that had been made in the past 25 years. The *Washington Post* of February 18, 1988, printed their letters.

Afro-Americans have come a long way considering what they have had to deal with. Although they have come far, they still have a long way to go. Dr. King had a dream, and in his memory we should further the process of eliminating [doing away with] racial discrimination.

One way to improve conditions is to teach students, Black and White, about the Afro-American heritage—not just about slavery, but about figures in literature and politics. We need to do this more than once a year, too. It's done in February and then drifts away until next year.

Increasing understanding would convince more people that Blacks are worth more than some credit us for.

—Aisha Satterwhite

My dad has told me of not being able to get into a restaurant because he is an Afro-American. I have seen stories on television of how Blacks used to be banned from everyday activities. Today, you can easily find a restaurant owned by a Black person.

At the beginning of the Civil Rights Movement, there weren't any Black Supreme Court Justices. There weren't any Black people running for President. A Black man could be beaten up in his own home and his [attacker] could get away unpunished.

The accomplishments in the last 25 years are remarkable. What is equally important is the [determination] of Black people in maintaining their equal status. Although we have not reached the totally integrated society that Martin Luther King Jr. and others dreamed of, we are well on our way.

—Adrian Fenty

1. The writer of the first letter thinks that one way to improve conditions is to

_____

2. The writer of the second letter thinks that Blacks are determined to _____

_____

# CHAPTER REVIEW: CRITICAL THINKING

The United States has one of the lowest voting rates of any democratic country. In the election of 1984, about 56 percent of Black adults voted. Young people vote less than older people.

1. Why do you think so many people do not vote? _____

_____

2. What reasons can you give for a person to vote? _____

_____

# UNIT 5 REVIEW

## Summary of the Unit

A few of the important events and facts presented in Unit 5 are listed below. Write these events and facts in your notebook and add three more.

1. Since the Voting Rights Act, many more Blacks have been elected to office.
2. More Blacks have entered the middle class. However, inner cities still have serious problems of poverty.
3. Blacks have many accomplishments in the arts and sports.
4. Black Americans continue to strive for equality.
5. Black educators and leaders encourage Black youths to stay in school so they can gain the skills and education they need for good jobs and careers.

## Understanding What You Have Read

Choose each correct answer and write the letter in the space provided.

_____ 1. The first Black to be elected mayor of a major American city was
    a. Jesse Jackson.
    b. Carl Stokes.
    c. Andrew Young.

_____ 2. The Black members of Congress have formed a group called the
    a. Congressional Black Caucus.
    b. House of Representatives.
    c. Budget Committee.

_____ 3. Education has made it possible for Blacks to
    a. move into good paying jobs.
    b. become professionals.
    c. both a and b.

_____ 4. Today, Black athletes take part in
    a. few sports.
    b. almost all major league sports.
    c. only the sport of basketball.

_____ 5. A sizable number of Blacks today are in the
    a. middle class.
    b. underclass.
    c. upper class.

_____ 6. Black Americans have succeeded
    a. only in sports and show business.
    b. in all areas of American life.
    c. only in business and college.

## Building Your Vocabulary

Choose one of the words below to complete each of the following sentences.

president    Breadbasket    Robert Weaver    Mitchell    Thurgood Marshall
Dunham    Doug Williams    Walker    service

_____ 1. _____ is the only Black member of the United States Supreme Court.

_____ 2. In 1972, Shirley Chisholm ran for the office of _____.

_____ 3. Jesse Jackson's Operation _____ was to develop greater job opportunities for Blacks.

_____ 4. Katherine _____ created a type of dance based on African, Caribbean, and American dances.

_____ 5. The first Black to hold a cabinet post was _____.

_____ 6. The founder and director of the Dance Theatre of Harlem is Arthur _____.

_____ 7. _____ work is growing in the United States as manufacturing work declines.

_____ 8. _____ of the Washington Redskins was the first Black quarterback to lead his team to victory in the Super Bowl.

_____ 9. *The Color Purple* was written by Alice _____.

## Developing Ideas and Skills

Study the graph. Then decide whether or not each sentence is true. If the sentence is true, write **T** next to it. If it is false, write **F** and rewrite the sentence to make it true.

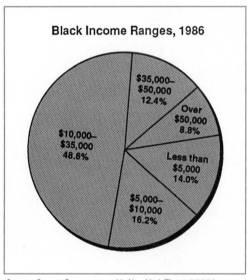

**Black Income Ranges, 1986**

$35,000–$50,000 12.4%

Over $50,000 8.8%

$10,000–$35,000 48.6%

Less than $5,000 14.0%

$5,000–$10,000 16.2%

*Source:* Census Bureau, quoted in New York Times, 2/29/88

_____ 1. The smallest percentage of Blacks make between $10,000 and $35,000.

_____

_____ 2. The percentage of Blacks who make between $35,000 and $50,000 is 17.5 percent.

_____

_____ 3. Less than 10 percent of Blacks make over $50,000.

_____

## Making History Live

1. Read a novel or book of poems by one of the Black writers discussed in the unit. What does this person's work tell you about the Black experience?
2. Report on one of the performers, political leaders, writers, or personalities discussed in this unit. Which one would you choose as a role model and why?

# Glossary _____

**affirmative action** the preferential hiring of Blacks and other minorities to make up for past discrimination (p. 68)

**Black Muslims** followers of Elijah Muhammad (p. 66)

**Black Renaissance** a flowering of Black art and thought that reached a peak in the 1920s (p. 28)

**blues** songs that express sadness or loneliness (p. 10)

**boll weevil** an insect harmful to the cotton plant (p. 24)

**boycott** a group refusal to buy or use something in order to influence others (p. 6)

**cakewalk** a lively dance contest having a cake as a prize (p. 11)

**CIO** initials of the Congress of Industrial Organizations, a group of labor unions (p. 34)

**Cotton Club** a popular Harlem nightclub first opened in 1927 (p. 29)

**depression** an economic slowdown resulting in unemployment and hardship (p. 34)

**dissent** to disagree (p. 2)

**exodus** movement of a group from a place (p. 6)

**Exodusters** Blacks who left the South in the 1870s to settle in Kansas (p. 6)

**ghetto** an overcrowded neighborhood where people of a certain group are forced to live as a result of unfair housing practices elsewhere (p. 24)

**Great Depression** a period of economic slowdown in the 1930s with high unemployment (p. 34)

**Great Migration** the movement of over one million Blacks from the South to cities in the North and West between 1915 and 1925 (p. 24)

**integrate** bring together into one group (p. 52)

**jazz** rhythmic American music played with varying amounts of improvisation (p. 27)

**Jim Crow laws** state laws passed after the Civil War that legalized segregation of Blacks and Whites (p. 2)

**journalist** a reporter or broadcaster who deals with the news (p. 85)

**labor union** a workers' organization interested in better wages and working conditions (p. 34)

**lynching** mob killings (especially hangings) of people (p. 2)

**Medicaid** a government program that pays the health care costs of needy individuals (p. 68)

**middle class** the social class whose members are neither rich nor poor (p. 46)

**militant** a person who seeks political change by force if necessary (p. 60)

**NAACP** initials of the National Association for the Advancement of Colored People, a Black political action group formed in 1910 (p. 16)

**National Urban League** a Black political action group formed in 1911 to seek improvements for Blacks living in American cities (p. 16)

**New Deal** government programs to promote economic recovery and social reform in the 1930s. Begun by President Franklin D. Roosevelt. (p. 38)

**Niagara Movement** a group formed in 1905 to seek better rights for Blacks (p. 16)

**plasma** a part of the blood (p. 44)

**poll tax** a fee paid in order to vote (p. 2)

**prejudice** dislike of other people for their race, religion, or national origin (p. 6)

**primary** an election held by a political party to choose a candidate for public office (p. 16)

**professional** a person with a job requiring special education or training (p. 44)

**ragtime** music combining African and marching band rhythms (p. 19)

**Reconstruction** the period following the Civil War from 1865 to 1877 (p. 2)

**renaissance** a "rebirth" or flowering of culture and thought (p. 28)

**rent party** a party with an admission fee (p. 34)

**role model** a person one wishes to be like (p. 86)

**Savoy Ballroom** a popular entertainment center in Harlem in the 1930s and 1940s (p. 29)

**segregation** the separation of people by race, religion, or national origin (p. 2)

**service jobs** non-manufacturing jobs (p. 78)

**sit-in** the use by Blacks of seats in a racially segregated public place to protest racial discrimination (p. 56)

**sociologist** a social scientist who studies human societies (p. 45)

**spiritual** a kind of Black religious song (p. 10)

**transfusion** medical replacement of blood (p. 44)

**UNIA** initials for the Universal Negro Improvement Association, a group formed by Marcus Garvey to improve economic conditions of Blacks (p. 24)

**welfare** payments made by the government to the needy (p. 34)

# Index